# Plant Based Diet Cookbook for B

## Ignite Your Culinary Creativity with a Vibrant Veggie Voyage

Copyright © 2023
Sarah Roslin

# TABLE OF CONTENTS

# 1 INTRODUCTION

Welcome to the world of plant-based eating! In this Plant-Based Diet Cookbook, you'll discover a collection of delicious, nutrient-dense recipes that will not only tantalize your taste buds but also provide you with a multitude of health benefits.

A plant-based diet is a way of eating that focuses on whole, minimally processed plant foods. These include a colorful array of vegetables, fruits, whole grains, legumes, nuts, and seeds. By choosing to follow a plant-based diet, you'll be minimizing or eliminating animal products and heavily processed foods, which can lead to improved overall health and well-being.

The benefits of a plant-based diet extend beyond personal health. It is an environmentally friendly and sustainable choice that can help reduce greenhouse gas emissions, conserve water and land resources, and support a more ethical and compassionate approach to food production. Embracing this lifestyle is not only beneficial for your body but also for our planet.

Numerous scientific studies have linked plant-based diets to a reduced risk of chronic diseases, such as heart disease, diabetes, hypertension, and certain types of cancer. Additionally, this way of eating has been shown to promote healthy weight management, improved digestion, and increased energy levels.

I must emphasize the importance of being mindful of specific nutrients when following a plant-based diet. Paying attention to your intake of vitamin B12, iron, and omega-3 fatty acids is crucial, as these nutrients are less abundant in plant foods. To ensure adequate consumption, you may need to incorporate fortified foods or consider supplementation under the guidance of a healthcare professional.

Lastly, while it's true that more plant-based options are becoming available in grocery stores and restaurants, it's essential to keep an eye on the nutritional quality of these products. Many processed plant-based foods can be high in added sugars, sodium, and unhealthy fats. This cookbook will guide you through preparing wholesome, homemade meals that prioritize your health without sacrificing flavor.

Join me on this journey to discover the incredible flavors, textures, and nourishment that a plant-based diet has to offer. With each recipe, you'll be taking a step toward improved health, increased vitality, and a more sustainable future. Let's get started and unleash the power of plants together.

## 1.1  PLANT BASED DIET VS VEGAN DIET

A diet rich in fruits, vegetables, seeds, nuts and grains is a plant based diet. This diet contains smaller amounts of eggs, meat and dairy whereas, emphasizes on fiber intake and nutrient rich foods. On the other hand, a plant based diet that completely excludes animal products such as eggs, meat, dairy and honey is known as Vegan Diet. This diet also eliminates items derived from animal sources such as whey, casein and gelatin. A person on a plant based diet can still have fewer choices for animal products whereas, a person following a vegan diet completely eliminates animal products from their diet.

## 1.2  CHARACTERISTICS OF DIET GROUPS

**Vegetables:** There are many form of vegetables such as cruciferous vegetables, leafy greens and root vegetables. They are all great source of antioxidants, fiber, minerals and vitamins while being caloric deficit. There are plenty ways to have vegetables such as boiled, grilled, raw, steamed, roasted, sautéed and baked etc.

**Fruits:** Various forms of fruits include tropical, berries and citrus. They can be eaten as a dessert as they contain natural sweetness. Fruits are a rich source of fiber, antioxidants, vitaminutes and minerals.

**Whole Grains:** they are a rich source of insoluble fiber and complex carbohydrates. They fuel up the body and are available in various forms like barley, whole, wheat bread, oats, brown rice and quinoa.

**Legumes:** Beans, lentils, peas and chickpeas are all form of legumes. They are low in fat and rich in protein, complex carbohydrates, fiber and micronutrients.

**Nuts and Seeds:** They can be consumed in raw and roasted form and can be taken as snacks and added in smoothies for additional nutrition. They are a great source of high density lipoproteins, fiber, protein and some micronutrients. There is a wide range of nuts and seeds from almonds, pistachios, pine nuts and walnuts to pumpkin seeds, chia seeds and flax seeds.

## 1.3  PROS AND CONS OF PLANT BASED DIET

**PROS**

**Health Benefits:** This diet is very beneficial in promoting healthy weight and healthy digestion. It also reduces risk of heart diseases, diabetes mellitus and some sorts of cancers.

**Environmental Factors:** In comparison with animal products, plant diet is a sustainable option as it reduces greenhouse gas emission and carbon footprint.

**Animal Welfare:** Ethically to protect animal species and killing of innocent animals' people choose plant based diet.

**Variety:** This diet offers wide range of foods, various flavors and amazing textures and hence makes interesting mealtimes.

## CONS

**Nutritional Deficiencies:** Deficiency of iron, vitamin B12 and protein are very common in plant based diet. Hence, adequate nutrient dense meals and supplements are recommended.

**Social challenges:** Following a plant based diet may be little challenging s majority of restaurants may not have many plant based diet options. Whereas, peers around may also not support your dietary choices.

**Cooking and Meal Planning:** This diet requires proper planning of weekly meals to preparing a balanced grocery list etc.

**Expenses:** This diet can also be on a pricy side especially if you choose to go for organic options instead of processed foods.

## 1.4 PLANT BASED DIET VS KETO DIET

Keto and plant based diets are two completely different dietary practices with different health benefits and principles. Some of them are listed below.

**Macronutrient Composition:** A plant based diet emphasizes on complex carb, lean protein and healthy fats. Whereas, keto diet focuses on minimal carbohydrates typically upto 20%, moderate proteins and a high fat diet.

**Health Benefits:** Plant based diet reduces risk of type-2 diabetes mellitus, heart diseases and cancers. While keto diet promotes weight loss, enchances insulin metabolism and reduces symptom of neurological diseases such as epilepsy.

**Sustainability:** Plant based diet is more sustainable in terms of minimal processed foods, limitations to use animal products and lesser resources.

**Feasibility:** Restricted intake of carbohydrates in keto diet make it a little challenging. Whereas, proper planning from grocery to weekly menu is required.

## 1.5 PLANT BASED DIET VS MEDITERRANEAN DIET

Plant-based and Mediterranean diets are both healthy dietary patterns that emphasize the consumption of whole, nutrient-dense foods. However, there are some differences between these two approaches:

Both Mediterranean diet and Plant based diet are healthy eating ways, that highlight diets rich in whole grains and nutrient rich foods. Nevertheless, there are some different points:

**Micronutrient Composition:** A plant based diet is often completely deprived of animal based essential nutrients and is low in cholesterol and saturated fats. It mainly contains nuts, seeds, whole grains, fruits and vegetables. While Mediterranean diet is well known for its higher intake of legumes, fruits, vegetables and whole grains. It is also rich in essential fats, olive oil, fish, poultry and dairy.

**Focus on Specific Foods:** With the exception of some specific foods both Plant based diet and Mediterranean diet have fruits, vegetables, whole grains and legumes in common. Some foods that are specific to Mediterranean region are olives, tomatoes, onions, garlic, and capers. They are good for heart health and prevent other chronic conditions as they are rich in fiber, essential fats, and are a great source of antioxidants.

**Health Benefits:** Although both plant-based and Mediterranean diets are well known for their numerous healthy benefits, they manage diabetes and prevent cancers. But Mediterranean diet is essentially known for its heart healthy benefits and in reducing risks of heart disease. It also decreases inflammation and improves cognitive abilities.

**Sustainability:** Mediterranean diet is more flexible and sustainable than plant based diet, as it emphasizes on the social eating patterns, and is easier to adapt in different cultural practices. Plant based diet lacks variety.

## 1.6  PLANT BASED DIET VS LOW CARB DIET

Low-carb and plant-based diets are two distinct dietary strategies with special tenets and health advantages. The main distinctions between them are as follows:

**Macronutrient composition:** Consuming full, plant-based foods including vegetables, fruits, legumes, nuts, seeds, and whole grains is emphasized in a plant-based diet. Lean protein, healthy fats, and complex carbs are often present, along with maybe some animal products. On the other hand, a low-carb diet tends to be high in protein and good fats while restricting the intake of carbs, frequently to fewer than 50 grams per day.

**Health benefits:** Low-carb and plant-based diets both offer potential health advantages. A plant-based diet is linked to a decreased incidence of obesity, type 2 diabetes, some malignancies, and heart disease. Low-carb diets might aid in shedding pounds, lowering blood sugar and insulin levels, and lowering some heart disease risk factors.

**Sustainability:** As they emphasize entire, minimally processed foods and are better for the environment, plant-based diets are often seen as being more sustainable than low-carb diets. In order to create animal goods, which use more resources, low-carb diets frequently rely on them, making them unsuitable for vegetarians and vegans.

**Feasibility:** Low-carb and plant-based diets both take preparation and work to properly follow. For some people, especially those who are accustomed to ingesting large amounts of animal products, plant-based diets may be more difficult. Others may find low-carb diets difficult because they must pay close attention to their food choices to prevent vitamin shortages and because they may not be suitable for those with certain medical issues.

## 1.7 PLANT BASED DIET VS VEGETARIAN DIET

Both vegetarianism and plant-based eating habits place a heavy emphasis on plant-based meals. There are a few distinctions between them, though

**Definition:** A plant-based diet is a dietary regimen that places an emphasis on eating entire, plant-based foods and restricts or completely avoids animal products including meat, dairy, and eggs. On the other side, a vegetarian diet forbids meat but allows dairy, eggs, and other foods obtained from animals.

**Nutrient composition:** Vegetarian and plant-based diets can both be healthy, but careful planning is necessary to guarantee appropriate consumption of vital minerals such protein, iron, calcium, and vitamin B12. In order to satisfy dietary requirements, plant-based diets may be lower in protein and other micronutrients, such as vitamin B12 and iron. This may necessitate supplementation or careful food selection. Vegetarian diets could contain more dairy and eggs, which are sources of some of these nutrients.

**Health benefits:** Many health advantages, such as decreased risks of heart disease, diabetes, especially type 2 diabetes, and several malignancies, have been linked to plant-based and vegetarian diets. A well-designed plant-based diet, however, can provide extra health advantages because of its increased fiber and antioxidant content.

**Sustainability:** As they are eco-friendlier and need less resources to create, plant-based and vegetarianism diets are seen as being more sustainable than those that mainly rely on animal products. But, because they don't include any animal products, plant-based diets could be more environmentally friendly than vegetarian ones.

## 1.8 PLANT BASED DIET VS PALEO DIET

Both the plant-based and paleo genic diets have their own principles and health advantages. The main distinctions between them are as follows:

**Food choices:** An focus on entire, plant-based foods comprising vegetables, fruits, legumes, nuts, seeds, and whole grains is part of a plant-based diet, which may or may not also contain certain animal products. A paleo diet, in contrast, forgoes grains, dairy products, and processed foods in favor of foods that were accessible during the Prehistoric period, such as meat, fish, eggs, nuts, seeds, fruits, and vegetables.

**Macronutrient composition:** While paleo diets place a concentrate on high levels of protein and good fats and may be lower in carbs, plant-based diets typically contain complex carbohydrates, healthy fats, and lean protein.

**Health benefits:** Paleo and plant-based diets both offer potential health benefits. A plant-based diet is linked to a decreased incidence of obesity, type 2 diabetes, some malignancies, and heart disease. Paleo diets may help with weight loss, better blood sugar homeostasis, and inflammation lowering.

**Sustainability:** Due to their concentration on complete, less processed foods and greater renewability, plant-based diets are often seen as being more ecological than paleo diets. Paleo diets may contain a lot of animal items; whose production uses more resources.

**Feasibility:** Paleo and plant-based diets both take preparation and work to effectively follow. While paleo diets may be more difficult for those who consume large amounts of grains and dairy products, plant-based diets may be more difficult for people who are used to eating large amounts of animal products.

# 2  EQUIPMENT USED IN PLANT BASED DIET

Some common kitchen equipment that can be used to make plant-based recipes are listed below:

1. **A blender** - is necessary for making sauces, nut butters, and smoothies.
2. **Food processor** - useful for blending nuts, seeds, and other ingredients for vegetarian burgers, spreads, and dips.
3. **A juicer** - is used to extract the juice out of fresh fruits and vegetables.
4. **Spiralizer** - for preparing sweet potato, zucchini or other vegetable-based noodles.
5. **A steamer basket** - is used to steam vegetables including green beans, broccoli, and carrots.
6. **A nonstick pan -** is useful for sautéing veggies like onions, peppers, and mushrooms.
7. **A baking sheet** - which is used to roast vegetables like cauliflower, Brussels sprouts, or sweet potatoes.
8. **A slow cooker** - may be used to prepare soups, stews, or chili using vegetables, beans, and lentils.
9. **A pressure cooker** - to swiftly cook grains, beans, and lentils.
10. **An air fryer** - may be used to make crunchy baked veggies or plant-based snacks.

You can generate a range of plant-based meals with the aid of these kitchen tools, which will also make meal preparation easier. It's important to keep in mind that you don't absolutely need all of them to enjoy a plant-based diet, and many plant-based meals can be made with basic cooking equipment and kitchen items like a knife and cutting board.

# 3 PERMITTED AND NON PERMITTED FOODS

In contrast to limiting or avoiding animal products and processed foods, a plant-based diet places an emphasis on the intake of whole, minimally processed plant foods. Following are some examples of items that are acceptable and prohibited in a plant-based diet:

**Permitted Foods:**

1. **Vegetables -** onions, garlic, carrots, beets, sweet potatoes, spinach, broccoli, spinach, and kale.
2. **Fruits** - including pineapple, kiwi, mango, apples, bananas, oranges, berries, and grapes.
3. **Legumes** - which include lentils, chickpeas, navy beans, kidney beans, and black beans.
4. **Whole Grains -** whole wheat bread, quinoa, brown rice, oats, and barley.
5. **Nuts and Seeds** - including pumpkin seeds, chia seeds, cashews, and walnuts.

6. **Plant Based Milk** - soy milk, coconut milk, and non-dairy yoghurt are among the plant-based milk and yoghurt options.

**Non-Permitted Foods:**

1. **Animal Products -** including dairy, eggs, fish, poultry, and meat.
2. **Fried meals -** chips, candies and sugary drinks are examples of processed foods.
3. **Refined carbs -** such as white pasta, bread, and rice.
4. **Heavily processed plant-based foods -** such as sweet desserts, vegan cheese, and meat substitutes made from plants.
5. **Added Oils -** high-fat plant-based products like coconut oil and refined vegetable oils like canola or sunflower oil.

## 3.1 REPLACEMENTS OF DAIRY AND MEAT

A number of nutrient-dense plant-based foods can be used to replace dairy and meat in a plant-based diet. These are a few instances:

### Dairy Replacement

- **Plant-Based Milk:** Use plant-based milk instead of cow's milk, such as oat, almond, soy, or coconut milk.
- **Non-Dairy Yogurt:** Choose for yoghurt produced without milk using soy, coconut, almond, or cashew milk.
- **Nutritional Yeast:** You may use nutritional yeast for cheese. It may be sprinkled on top of food and is used in sauces, dips, and has a nutty, cheesy flavour.
- **Cashew Cream:** To produce a creamy sauce or dip, blend cashews that have been soaked in water.

### Meat Replacement

- **Legumes:** Including legumes as a source of protein, such as beans, lentils, and chickpeas. They may be substituted for meat in burgers and tacos as well as soups, stews, and salads.
- **Tofu and tempeh:** These soy-based foods can be used in stir-fries, curries, and sandwiches in lieu of meat.
- **Seitan:** Composed of wheat protein, seitan has a chewy texture and may be used in sandwiches, pot pies, and stews in place of meat.
- **Mushrooms:** Use Portobello or shiitake mushrooms in place of beef in burgers or as a taco or fajita filler.

It's crucial to remember that a plant-based diet can change depending on personal tastes and dietary requirements. To make sure you're getting all the nutrients you need, it's advised to eat a range of nutrient-dense plant foods.

# 4  STORAGE

It's necessary to store plant-based foods properly to preserve their nutritional content, quality, and freshness. Here are some pointers for effectively using your cupboard and refrigerator to keep plant-based foods:

**Refrigerator:**

- **Cold Zone:** The rear and bottom shelves of the refrigerator are its coldest locations. Perishable plant-based items including leafy greens, berries, and herbs are best kept at this location.
- **Moderate Zone:** The refrigerator's middle racks are in the moderate zone, which is ideal for preserving plant-based proteins like tofu, tempeh, and veggie burgers.
- **Humid Zone:** The refrigerator's bottom drawers are made to create a humid atmosphere, which is ideal for preserving produce like carrots, celery, and broccoli.
- **Avert overcrowding:** An overcrowded refrigerator may have inadequate air circulation, which might hasten the deterioration of the food. To ensure optimal airflow, provide some space between objects.

**Pantry:**

- **Dry storage:** refers to keeping dried plant-based goods like grains, pasta and nuts in a cold, dry location like a pantry or closet.
- **Cold and Dark:** A pantry or basement is an excellent storage space since some fruits and vegetables, such as potatoes, onions and winter squash, like a chilly and dark environment.
- **Airtight containers:** To keep grains, nuts and dried fruits fresh and prevent them from getting rancid, store opened packages in airtight containers.
- **Label and organize:** Maintain organization in your pantry by labelling your containers and assembling like-items-together groups. This will lessen food waste and make it simpler to find the supplies you require.

You can make sure that your plant-based food stays tasty and nutrient-dense for longer by paying attention to these suggestions.

# 5  FAQ

**How do you cook plant-based meals that are satisfying and yet flavorful?**

Cooking plant-based meals that are satisfying and flavorful can be achieved by using a variety of herbs, spices, and cooking techniques. Experiment with different combinations of herbs and spices to create bold and unique flavors. Using ingredients like garlic, ginger, cumin, and chili can add depth and complexity to your dishes. Try roasting, grilling, or sautéing your vegetables to add caramelization and texture. Incorporating healthy fats like avocado or nuts can also enhance the flavor and texture of your meals.

**What are most of the best plant-based sources for building muscles?**

Some of the best plant-based sources for building muscles are beans, lentils, tofu, tempeh, quinoa, and nuts. These foods are high in protein, essential amino acids, and other nutrients that are necessary for muscle growth and repair. Additionally, incorporating a variety of fruits and vegetables can provide antioxidants and vitaminutes that can support muscle recovery and overall health.

**What are some plant-based options for breakfast?**

Plant-based options for breakfast can include oatmeal, smoothie bowls, chia pudding, tofu scramble, avocado toast, and fruit salads. These options are nutrient-dense, high in fiber, and can provide sustained energy throughout the day. You can also experiment with adding different fruits, nuts, and seeds to create new and exciting breakfast combinations.

**How can a plant-based diet improve mental health?**

A plant-based diet can improve mental health by providing essential nutrients like omega-3 fatty acids, vitaminutes, and minerals that support brain function and reduce inflammation. Additionally, plant-based diets are typically high in fiber, which can improve gut health and support the gut-brain axis. Studies have also shown that plant-based diets can reduce symptoms of depression and anxiety and improve overall mood and well-being.

**Can a plant-based diet help with weight loss?**

Yes, a plant-based diet can help with weight loss. Plant-based diets tend to be high in fiber, low in saturated fat, and rich in nutrients, which can support weight loss and weight management. Additionally, plant-based diets typically include more whole foods and fewer processed foods, which can lead to a reduction in calorie intake and promote healthy eating habits.

**Are there any specific nutrients to pay attention to on a vegan diet?**

Some nutrients that may require attention on a vegan diet include vitamin B12, iron, calcium, zinc, and omega-3 fatty acids. These nutrients can be obtained from fortified foods or supplements, or by incorporating a variety of whole foods into your diet. It's important to consult with a healthcare professional or registered dietitian to ensure that you are meeting your nutrient needs on a vegan diet.

### How do you manage cravings and emotional eating on a plant-based diet?

To manage cravings and emotional eating on a plant-based diet, it's important to plan ahead and have healthy snacks readily available. Incorporating a variety of flavors and textures into your meals can also help satisfy cravings and prevent overeating. Mindful eating practices, such as taking time to chew slowly and savor your food, can also help reduce the likelihood of emotional eating.

### Can a plant-based diet help with chronic inflammation?

Yes, a plant-based diet can help with chronic inflammation. Plant-based diets are typically high in anti-inflammatory foods like fruits, vegetables, whole grains, and healthy fats. These foods contain antioxidants and other nutrients that can reduce inflammation and support overall health. Studies have also shown that plant-based diets can reduce the risk of chronic diseases that are associated with inflammation, such as heart disease and certain types of cancer.

### What is a plant-based diet?

A plant-based diet emphasizes whole, minimally processed foods derived from plants such as vegetables, fruits, whole grains, legumes, nuts, and seeds. It limits or excludes animal products like meat, dairy, and eggs.

### Why choose a plant-based diet?

People may choose a plant-based diet for various reasons, including health, ethical, and environmental concerns. Some research suggests that a plant-based diet can lower the risk of chronic diseases such as heart disease, diabetes, and some cancers.

### What are the benefits of a plant-based diet?

A plant-based diet can provide numerous benefits, including improved heart health, weight management, and digestive health. It may also lower the risk of certain chronic diseases, boost immune function, and promote overall well-being.

### Can you get enough protein on a plant-based diet?

Yes, it is possible to get enough protein on a plant-based diet. Protein can be obtained from sources such as beans, lentils, tofu, tempeh, nuts, and seeds.

### What are some common nutrient deficiencies in a plant-based diet?

Common nutrient deficiencies in a plant-based diet include vitamin B12, iron, calcium, zinc, and omega-3 fatty acids. However, these can be easily addressed with a balanced and varied plant-based diet or supplements.

**Can a plant-based diet be affordable?**

Yes, a plant-based diet can be affordable. In fact, many plant-based foods are more affordable than animal products. Shopping for seasonal produce, buying in bulk, and cooking at home can help save money.

**Is a plant-based diet suitable for athletes?**

Yes, a plant-based diet can be suitable for athletes. Plant-based sources of protein, carbohydrates, and healthy fats can provide the necessary fuel for athletic performance and recovery.

**Can children follow a plant-based diet?**

Yes, children can follow a plant-based diet with proper planning and guidance to ensure adequate nutrient intake for growth and development.

**What are some examples of plant-based protein sources?**

Plant-based protein sources include beans, lentils, tofu, tempeh, nuts, seeds, quinoa, and whole grains.

**How do you ensure you're getting enough calcium on a plant-based diet?**

Calcium can be obtained from plant-based sources such as leafy greens, fortified plant milks, fortified tofu, and sesame seeds. Calcium supplements can also be taken if necessary.

**What are some easy plant-based meal ideas?**

Easy plant-based meal ideas include veggie stir-fries, grain bowls, salads, soups, pasta dishes, and veggie burgers.

**What are some common plant-based substitutes for meat, dairy, and eggs?**

Common plant-based substitutes for meat include tofu, tempeh, and seitan. For dairy, plant-based milks, yogurts, and cheeses made from nuts, soy, or coconut are available. For eggs, flax or chia seeds, tofu, and vegan egg substitutes can be used.

**Is a plant-based diet suitable for people with dietary restrictions or allergies?**

Yes, a plant-based diet can be suitable for people with dietary restrictions or allergies. It can be adapted to meet various dietary needs and preferences.

**Can you lose weight on a plant-based diet?**

Yes, a plant-based diet can support weight loss. It is often high in fiber and low in saturated fat, which can promote feelings of fullness and reduce calorie intake.

**How do you handle social situations and dining out on a plant-based diet?**

Transitioning to a plant-based diet can be challenging when it comes to social situations and dining out, but there are ways to handle it. One option is to research restaurants beforehand and look for plant-based options on the menu. It's also helpful to communicate your dietary preferences to the host or server in advance. You can also offer to bring a plant-based dish to share at gatherings or suggest plant-based restaurants to your friends. Remember that it's okay to stick to your dietary choices, and don't be afraid to ask for modifications to menu items to make them plant-based.

**What are some tips for transitioning to a plant-based diet?**

Some tips for transitioning to a plant-based diet include gradually increasing the amount of plant-based foods in your meals, experimenting with new plant-based recipes, and finding plant-based alternatives to your favorite animal-based foods.

**How do you deal with cravings for meat and dairy when starting a plant-based diet?**

To deal with cravings for meat and dairy when starting a plant-based diet, try finding plant-based alternatives that satisfy the same cravings, such as vegan burgers or dairy-free ice cream. It can also be helpful to remind yourself of the reasons why you decided to adopt a plant-based diet.

**What are some plant-based sources of iron and calcium?**

Plant-based sources of iron include dark leafy greens, legumes, nuts and seeds, and fortified cereals. Plant-based sources of calcium include dark leafy greens, tofu, fortified plant milks, and nuts and seeds.

**What are some common myths about the plant-based diet?**

Common myths about the plant-based diet include that it is difficult to get enough protein, that it is expensive, and that it is not suitable for athletes or pregnant women. However, with proper planning and education, a plant-based diet can be nutritionally adequate for individuals of all ages and lifestyles.

**How do your meal plan for a plant-based diet?**

Meal planning for a plant-based diet involves incorporating a variety of whole plant foods such as grains, legumes, vegetables, fruits, and nuts and seeds. It can also be helpful to batch cook meals and snacks for the week.

**How do you deal with family or friends who are not supportive of a plant-based diet?**

When dealing with family or friends who are not supportive of a plant-based diet, try to educate them about the benefits and reasons behind your choice. You can also offer to cook a plant-based meal for them or bring your own food to gatherings.

**Can you still enjoy eating out on a plant-based diet?**

It is possible to enjoy eating out on a plant-based diet by researching restaurants ahead of time and choosing plant-based options on the menu or requesting modifications. It can also be helpful to bring your own snacks or meals when dining out.

**What are some delicious plant-based snacks?**

Delicious plant-based snacks include fresh fruit, vegetable sticks with hummus or nut butter, roasted chickpeas, trail mix, and vegan energy bars.

**What can I use for substitute for eggs in baking?**

There are several options for replacing eggs in the baking, including mashed bananas, applesauce, pumpkin puree, silken tofu or commercial egg replacer. The exact substitute will completely depend on the recipe and the desired outcome.

# 6  SHOPPING LIST FOR A WEEK

Here is a budget-friendly shopping list for one week of plant-based meals for an individual:

## Fruits and Vegetables

- Bananas – 7
- Apples – 7
- Oranges – 7
- Carrots – 1 lb.
- Broccoli – 1 head
- Cauliflower – 1 head

- Baby spinach – 1 bag
- Kale – 1
- Bell Pepper – 1
- Onion – 1
- Garlic – 1 head
- Avocado – 1

## Grains:

- Brown rice – 1 lb.
- Quinoa – 1 lb.

- Whole wheat pasta – 1 lb

## Canned/boxed goods:

- Black beans – 1 can
- Chickpeas – 1 can

- Diced tomatoes – 1 can
- Marinara sauce – 1 jar

## Nuts/Seeds:

- Almonds – ½ cup
- Cashews – ½ cup

- Chia seeds – ¼ cup

## Spices/Seasonings:

- Salt
- Pepper
- Garlic powder

- Onion powder
- Chili powder
- Cumin

## Beverages:

- Tea bags of your choice – 7
- Almond milk – ½ gallon

- Orange juice – ½ gallon

**Snacks:**

- Bag of popcorn – 1
- Bag of pretzels – 1
- Bag of trail mix – 1

# 7  BREAKFAST

## 7.1  Whole wheat Pancakes

Preparation Time - 5 minutes | Cooking Time - 8 minutes | Serves – 2

**Ingredients:**

- Flaxseeds – 1 tbsp. (7.5g)
- Water – 3 tbsp. (45ml)
- Whole wheat flour – 4 oz. (114g)
- Milk – ½ cup (118ml)
- Apple sauce – 2 tbsp. (30ml)
- Banana – ½ cup (120g)
- For Dressing:
- Banana chunks – 2 tbsp. (20g)
- Chocolate syrup – 2 tsp (10ml)

**Method:**

1. Let the mixture of ground flaxseed and water sit for a few minutes.
2. Blend all ingredients until smooth batter is formed
3. Pour the batter on greased skillet using a large spoon, according to the size of pancake you desire
4. Cook each side for about 2 minutes or until done on medium flame
5. Serve with banana and chocolate topping

**Nutrition per serving:**

Calories – 327 | Fat - 4.9g | Carbs - 65.2g | Protein - 11.4g | Potassium - 694mg | Cholesterol – 0mg | Sugar – 17.6g | Sodium – 256mg | Fiber – 10.6g

## 7.2  Classic French Toast

Preparation Time - 5 minutes | Cooking Time - 5 minutes | Serves 1

**Ingredients:**

- White bread – 2 slice
- Flaxseeds – 1 tbsp. (7.5g)
- Water – 3 tbsp. (45ml)
- Milk – ½ cup (118ml)
- Honey – 2 tbsp. (42g)
- Butter – 2 tsp (9.26g)

**Method:**

1. Preheat your skillet and grease it with butter.
2. Let the mixture of ground flaxseed and water sit for a few minutes.
3. Mix eggs, milk and honey.
4. Dip the bread slices in mixture and pour on the skillet
5. Cook each side for 1 min
6. Serve with any topping you desire

**Nutrition per serving:**

Calories – 498 | Fat - 21.5g | Carbs - 61.9g | Protein - 17.4g | Potassium - 349mg | Cholesterol – 240mg | Sugar – 29.4g | Sodium – 489mg | Fiber – 5.7g

## 7.3  Oatmeal with nuts and fruits

Preparation Time - 5 minutes| Cooking Time - 0 minutes| Serves 1

**Ingredients:**

- Oats – ½ cup (45g)
- Water – ½ cup (118ml)
- Almond milk – ⅓ cup (79ml)
- Sliced strawberries & apples – ½ cup (75g)
- Diced walnuts & almonds – 2 tbsp. (15g)

**Method:**

1. Soak oatmeal in water for 10 minutes
2. Drain the excess water if left
3. Add almond milk with oatmeal to a bowl
4. Top it with fruits & nuts

**Nutrition per serving:**

Calories – 334| Fat - 14g | Carbs - 43g |Protein - 10g | Potassium - 379mg | Cholesterol – 0mg |Sugar – 10g |Sodium – 79mg |Fiber – 9g

## 7.4  Avocado Toast

Preparation Time - 3 minutes| Cooking Time - 0 minutes| Serves 1

**Ingredients:**

- Avocado – 1 medium sized
- Whole wheat bread – 2 slice
- Cherry tomatoes – 2

**Method:**

1. Toast bread slices
2. Spread mashed avocado on the slices
3. Top it with slices of tomatoes

**Nutrition per serving:**

Calories – 415| Fat - 22.2g | Carbs - 46.7g |Protein - 11.7g | Potassium - 1145mg | Cholesterol – 0mg |Sugar – 7.6g |Sodium – 341mg |Fiber – 14.2g

## 7.5  Oats & Chia seeds pudding

Preparation Time - 7 minutes | Cooking Time - 0 minutes | Serves 1

**Ingredients:**

- Rolled Oats – ½ cup (45g)
- Chia seeds (soaked overnight) – 2 tbsp. (25g)
- Water – ½ cup (118ml)
- Soy milk – ⅓ cup (79g)
- Diced apples & mango – ½ cup (75g)
- Diced nuts – 2 tbsp. (15g)

**Method:**

1. Soak rolled oats in water for 10 minutes
2. Drain the excess water
3. Add almond milk with oats and chia seeds to a bowl
4. Top it with fruits & nuts

**Nutrition per serving:**

Calories – 344 | Fat - 15g | Carbs - 43g | Protein - 12g | Potassium - 441mg | Cholesterol – 0mg | Sugar – 10g | Sodium – 68mg | Fiber – 12g

## 7.6  Scrambled Tofu & Mushroom Omelet

Preparation Time - 5 minutes | Cooking Time - 3 minutes | Serves 1

**Ingredients:**

- Tofu – 3 oz.(85g)
- Diced Vegetables (onions, tomatoes, spinach) – ½ cup (80g)
- Salt – as required
- Cumin – 1 tsp (2g)
- Sliced mushrooms – 2 tbsp. (10g)
- Black pepper – 1 tsp (2.3g)
- Coconut oil – 2 tsp (10ml)
- Mint leaves – 2-3

**Method:**

1. Blend tofu add spices, mushrooms and vegetables to it, mix well
2. Pour oil on the skillet
3. Pour the batter and scramble
4. Serve with mint leaves on top

**Nutrition per serving:**

Calories – 198 | Fat - 15g | Carbs - 5g | Protein - 12g | Potassium - 430mg | Cholesterol – 0mg | Sugar – 1g | Sodium – 168mg | Fiber – 2g

## 7.7 Banana & Peanut butter Muffins

Preparation Time - 10 minutes | Cooking Time - 25 minutes | Serves 3

**Ingredients:**

- Ripe banana (mashed) – ½ cup (120g)
- Vegetable oil – ½ cup (96ml)
- All purpose flour – 1 cup (125g)
- Baking powder – 2 tsp (10g)
- Almond milk – ½ cup (118ml)
- Brown sugar – ⅔ cup (135g)
- Peanut butter – 2 tbsp. (32g)
- Chocolate chips – ½ cup (90g)

**Method:**

1. Heat oven at 200C (180F)
2. Line 2 muffin trays, grease them and place butter paper
3. Mix flour, sugar and baking powder
4. Add to it banana, milk, oil and other ingredients, beat firmly
5. Fill muffin cases two-thirds, and bake for 20-25 minutes, or until risen
6. Serve with coffee

**Nutrition per serving:**

Calories – 637 | Fat - 35g | Carbs - 74g | Protein - 10g | Potassium - 370mg | Cholesterol – 0mg | Sugar – 39g | Sodium – 320mg | Fiber – 4g

## 7.8 Avocado & Chickpea pancakes

Preparation Time - 10 minutes | Cooking Time - 7 minutes | Serves 3

**Ingredients:**

- Avocado – 1 medium sized
- Chickpeas – ½ cup (82g)
- Yogurt – ½ cup (120g)
- Salt – pinch
- Paprika – 1 tsp (2g)
- Black pepper – 2 tsp (6g)
- Butter – 2 tsp (10g)
- Spinach – 2 tbsp. (6g)
- For topping:
- Olives (sliced) – 2 tbsp. (14g)
- Cherry tomatoes (diced) – 2 tbsp. (20g)

**Method:**

1. Boil chickpeas until softened
2. Mash chickpeas with avocado
3. Add yogurt and spices to the mixture
4. Pour the batter on greased skillet using a large spoon, according to the size of pancake you desire
5. Cook each side for about 2 minutes or until done on medium flame
6. Top the pancakes with olives and tomatoes
7. Serve with mint sauce

**Nutrition per serving:** Calories – 295 | Fat - 18g | Carbs - 23g | Protein - 11g | Potassium - 609mg | Cholesterol – 10mg | Sugar – 2g | Sodium – 150mg | Fiber – 9g

## 7.9   Fruity Quinoa Bowl

Preparation Time - 5 minutes | Cooking Time - 10 minutes | Serves 1

**Ingredients:**

- Quinoa (cooked) – ½ cup (85g)
- Almond milk – ½ cup (120ml)
- Cinnamon – pinch
- Chia seeds – 2 tbsp. (20g)
- Peanut butter – 2 tbsp. (32g)
- Strawberries (sliced) – 3
- Blueberries – ½ cup (75g)
- Banana (sliced) – 1 medium sized

**Method:**

1. Rinse quinoa in a fine mesh strainer under cold water until water runs clear.
2. In a saucepan, combine quinoa, 1 cup of water, and a pinch of cinnamon. Bring to a boil, then reduce heat to low, cover, and simmer for 15 minutes or until the quinoa is cooked and the water is absorbed.
3. In a separate saucepan, heat almond milk and peanut butter over low heat, stirring until the mixture is smooth and well combined.
4. Add cooked quinoa to the almond milk and peanut butter mixture, then stir in chia seeds.
5. Transfer the quinoa mixture to a bowl and top with sliced strawberries, blueberries, and banana.

**Nutrition per serving:** Calories – 497 | Fat - 20g | Carbs - 67g | Protein - 17g | Potassium - 906mg | Cholesterol – 0mg | Sugar – 22g | Sodium – 184mg | Fiber – 15g

## 7.10 Scrambled Tofu Wrap

Preparation Time - 3 minutes | Cooking Time - 0 minutes | Serves 1

**Ingredients:**

- Tofu – 2oz (57g)
- Avocado – ½ medium sized
- Whole wheat tortillas – 1
- Spinach (boiled) – 2 tbsp. (30g)
- Red pepper – 1 tsp (1.8g)
- Salt – pinch
- Mayonnaise – 0.5 oz (15g)
- Hummus – 1 tbsp. (15g)
- Cherry tomato (sliced) – 1
- Vegetable oil – 1 tsp (5ml)

**Method:**

1. Mash avocado, spinach and tofu and scramble them with oil
2. Add spices
3. Place the scrambled tofu mixture in the tortilla
4. Drizzle over the mayonnaise and hummus, and top with tomato
5. Wrap the tortilla and serve with tomato sauce

**Nutrition per serving:**

Calories – 385 | Fat - 24g | Carbs - 31g | Protein - 15g | Potassium - 737mg | Cholesterol – 0mg | Sugar – 3g | Sodium – 437mg | Fiber – 11g

## 7.11 Tofu Omelet with Mushrooms & Olives

Preparation Time - 5 minutes | Cooking Time - 3 minutes | Serves 1

**Ingredients:**

- Tofu – 3oz (85g)
- Tomatoes – 2 tbsp. (18g)
- Onions – 2 tbsp. (20g)
- Mushrooms (sliced) – 1
- Black olives (sliced) – 1 tbsp (6g)
- Green chilies – 1 tbsp. (5g)
- Salt – as required
- Soy sauce – 2 tsp (10ml)

**Method:**

1. Blend tofu, mix with vegetables and spices
2. Pour the mixture on a skillet and make omelet
3. Serve with toast

**Nutrition per serving:**

Calories – 156 | Fat - 10g | Carbs - 6g | Protein - 13g | Potassium - 294mg | Cholesterol – 0mg | Sugar – 2g | Sodium – 561mg | Fiber – 2g

## 7.12 Avocado & Chickpea Sandwich

Preparation Time - 10 minutes | Cooking Time - 2 minutes | Serves 1

**Ingredients:**

- Chickpea – 1 oz (28g)
- Avocado – 1 medium sized
- Whole wheat bread – 2 slice
- Tomatoes – 1 medium sized
- Lettuce – 2-3 leaves
- Mayonnaise – 1 tbsp. (15g)
- Olive oil – 1 tsp (5ml)
- Black pepper – 2 tsp (6g)
- Salt – according to taste

**Method:**

1. Toast bread slices
2. Spread mayonnaise over the slices and place lettuce leaves
3. Mix chickpeas with spices and olive oil
4. Spread mashed avocado on the slices
5. Top it with slices of tomatoes

**Nutrition per serving:**

Calories – 490 | Fat - 24g | Carbs - 56g | Protein - 16g | Potassium - 980mg | Cholesterol – 0mg | Sugar – 7g | Sodium – 530mg | Fiber – 18g

## 7.13 Avocado & Mushrooms Sandwich

Preparation Time - 10 minutes | Cooking Time - 3 minutes | Serves 1

**Ingredients:**

- Mushroom – 1
- Avocado – 1 medium sized
- Whole wheat bread – 2 slice
- Cheese slices – 2
- Tomato sauce – 1 tbsp (15ml)
- Onions – ½ medium sized
- Iceberg– 2-3 leaves
- Olive oil – 2 tsp (10ml)
- Red pepper – 2 tsp (6g)
- Salt – according to taste

**Method:**

1. Air fry mushroom slices with olive oil and spices for a minute or two (as preferred)
2. Toast bread slices
3. Spread tomato sauce over the slices and place iceberg
4. Spread mashed avocado on the slices
5. Place mushrooms over the avocado
6. Top it with slices of tomatoes, onions and cheese slices
7. Heat it the sandwich on low flame until cheese melts
8. Serve hot!

**Nutrition per serving:**

Calories – 502 | Fat - 31g | Carbs - 38g | Protein - 18g | Potassium - 1055mg | Cholesterol – 46mg | Sugar – 8g | Sodium – 762mg | Fiber – 11g

## 7.14 Chickpea Cupcakes

Preparation Time - 10 minutes | Cooking Time - 25 minutes | Serves 3

**Ingredients:**

- Chickpea flour – 1 cup (92g)
- Almond milk – ½ cup (120ml)
- Water – ½ cup (118ml)
- Nutritional yeast – 2 tsp (5g)
- Red pepper – 2 tsp (6g)
- Salt – 2 tsp (10g)
- Turmeric – 1 tsp (2.5g)
- For topping
- Vegetables – (tomatoes, onions, corn)

**Method:**

1. Mix almond milk in water and add yeast
2. Add the mixture to flour and fold
3. Add spices
4. Pour the mixture in greased cupcake tray
5. Add different toppings of your choice on cupcakes
6. Bake for 20-25 minutes at 180°C (356°F)

**Nutrition per serving:**

Calories – 221 | Fat - 4.4g | Carbs - 33.2g | Protein - 12.1g | Potassium - 459mg | Cholesterol – 0mg | Sugar – 3.6g | Sodium – 1429mg | Fiber – 9.1g

# 7.15 Avocado & Hash Brown Buns

Preparation Time - 7 minutes | Cooking Time - 0 minutes | Serves 2

**Ingredients:**

- Hash browns – 2
- Buns (of choice) – 2
- Avocado – 1 medium sized
- Tomatoes – 2 medium sized
- Lettuce leaves – 4
- Onions – 1 medium sized
- Thousand island – 2 tbsp. (30g)
- Mayonnaise – 2 tbsp. (30g)
- Tomato sauce – 2 tbsp. (30g)

**Method:**

1. Toast buns on low flame
2. Spread sauces and mashed avocado on both sides
3. Place lettuce leaves and Hash browns on flat side of buns
4. Top it with slices of onions and tomatoes (drizzle any sauces of choice)
5. Place the round side of buns on top

**Nutrition per serving:**

Calories – 494 | Fat - 37g | Carbs - 54g | Protein - 10g | Potassium - 900mg | Cholesterol – 12mg | Sugar – 9g | Sodium – 680mg | Fiber – 12g

# 7.16 Gram flour Tortillas

Preparation Time - 2 minutes | Cooking Time - 30 minutes | Serves 3

**Ingredients:**

- Gram four – ½ cup (58g)
- Water – as required
- Green onions (chopped) – 1 tbsp. (5g)
- Red pepper – 1 tsp (2g)
- Salt – pinch
- Vegetable oil – 1 tbsp. (15g)
- Cumin seeds – 1 tsp (2.5g)
- Dried fenugreek leaves – ½ tsp (0.5g)

**For Filling;**

- Baby spinach – 1 cup (30g)
- Butter – 1 tsp (5g)
- Onions (chopped) – 1 medium sized
- Cherry tomatoes (halved) – 5
- Red pepper – 1 tsp (2g)
- Salt – pinch
- Soy sauce – 2 tsp (10ml)
- Vinegar – 1 tsp (5ml)
- Paprika – 1 tsp (2g)

**Method:**

1. Whisk flour and water to make a smooth batter. Add spices and vegetables
2. On a skillet, brush ½ tsp of oil and pour batter. Spread it to a thin layer, to make tortillas. Add butter to a pan, sauté onions
3. Add spices and spinach and let it simmer until softened
4. Add tomatoes and cover it for another 2 minutes

5. Place the tortillas, add filling in one half and fold the other half. Serve with mint sauce

**Nutrition per serving:**

Calories – 173| Fat - 10.1g | Carbs - 15.6g |Protein - 5.6g | Potassium - 300mg | Cholesterol – 7.6mg |Sugar – 3.8g |Sodium – 194mg |Fiber – 3.5g

## 7.17 Carrot & Sweet potato Waffles

Preparation Time - 7 minutes| Cooking Time - 10 minutes| Serves 1

### Ingredients:

- Sweet potatoes (boiled) – 1 cup (200g)
- Carrots (finely grated) – ½ cup (50g)
- Almond milk – 3 oz (90ml)
- Corn starch – ¼ cup (32g)
- All-purpose flour – 1 cup (120g)
- Baking powder – 2 tsp (8.8g)
- Baking soda – ½ tsp (2.5g)
- Cinnamon – 1 tsp (2.6g)
- Salt – pinch
- Olive oil – for greasing
- Custard powder – ½ cup (64g)

### Method:

1. Grease both sides of preheat waffle iron
2. Blend all ingredients except the carrots
3. Transfer it to a bowl and fold in finely grated carrots
4. Pour the batter into the waffle trays to make 4 waffles
5. Cook for 4 minutes or until well done

6. Drizzle over honey or chocolate syrup
7. Serve with berries of choice

**Nutrition per serving:**

Calories – 93| Fat - 1g | Carbs - 9g |Protein - 12g | Potassium - 1694mg | Cholesterol – 0mg |Sugar – 2g |Sodium – 329mg |Fiber – 17.5g

## 7.18 Vegan Buckwheat Parfait

Preparation Time - 5 minutes| Cooking Time - 15 minutes| Serves – 4

### Ingredients

- Raw buckwheat groats – 1 cup (170g)
- Almond milk – 1 ½ cup (375ml)
- Maple syrup – 2 tbsp. (40ml)
- Vanilla extract – ½ tsp (2.5ml)
- Cinnamon powder – ¼ tsp (0.65g)
- Sea salt – ¼ tsp (1.5g)
- Mixed berries – 1 cup (145g)
- Walnuts – ¼ cup (30g)

### Method

1. After giving the buckwheat groats a cold water rinse, put them in a big dish. They should soak for at least 30 minutes or overnight in a covered container of water.
2. Buckwheat groats are once again drained and rinsed. The buckwheat, plant-based milk, maple syrup, vanilla extract, cinnamon, and sea salt should all be combined in a pot. When the buckwheat is soft and the liquid has been absorbed, bring to a boil, then decrease the heat to low and simmer for 10 to 15 minutes.
3. Let the buckwheat come to room temperature before layering it in

jars or glasses with the various berries and chopped almonds.

4. Immediately serve, or chill until ready to eat.

**Nutrition per serving:**

Calories - 252| Fat - 8g | Carbs - 41g |Protein - 7g |Potassium - 485mg | Cholesterol – 0mg |Sugar – 13g |Sodium – 158mg |Fiber – 9.3g

## 7.19 Granola Yogurt Parfait

Preparation Time - 5 minutes| Cooking Time - 0 minutes| Serves – 4

### Ingredients

- Vegan yogurt – 1 cup (240g)
- Granola – ½ cup (56g)
- Fresh mixed berries – ½ cup (70g)
- Chopped mixed nuts – ¼ cup (30g)

### Method

1. Put some granola at the bottom of a glass.
2. The vegan yoghurt should be topped with a coating of granola.
3. To the yoghurt, add a layer of mixed berries.
4. After placing a layer of berries, add more granola on top.
5. On top of the granola, spread out another layer of yoghurt.
6. the yoghurt with chopped almonds on top.
7. Serve right away.

**Nutrition per serving:** Calories - 380| Fat - 17g | Carbs - 48g |Protein - 11g | Potassium - 157mg | Cholesterol – 0mg |Sugar – 26g |Sodium – 120mg |Fiber – 10g

## 7.20 Vegan Sausages

Preparation Time: 10 minutes| Cooking Time: 25 minutes| Serving – 8

### Ingredients

- Cooked brown lentils – 1 cup (200g)
- Wheat gluten – ½ cup (52g)
- Nutritional yeast – ¼ cup (20g)
- Onion powder – 2 tsp (8g)
- Garlic powder – 2 tsp (8g)
- Dried sage – 1 tsp (1.5g)
- Dried thyme – 1 tsp (1.5g)
- Smoked paprika – ½ tsp (1.5g)
- Black pepper – ½ tsp (1.5g)
- Vegetable broth – ½ cup (120ml)
- Soy sauce – 2 tbsp (30ml)
- Maple syrup – 1 tbsp (15ml)

### Method

1. Set a baking sheet on your oven's 350°F (180°C) rack and preheat the oven.
2. Cooked lentils, essential wheat gluten, nutritional yeast, onion powder, garlic powder, dried sage, dried thyme, smoked paprika, and black pepper should all be combined in a large mixing dish.
3. Combine the vegetable broth, soy sauce, and maple syrup in a separate small bowl. Mix until a dough forms by adding the wet components to the dry ones.
4. Create eight banger patties out of the dough by dividing it into that number. Put the patties on the baking sheet that has been prepared.

5. The patties should be baked for 25 minutes, turning them over halfway through.

**Nutrition per serving:** Calories – 93 | Fat - 1g | Carbs - 9g | Protein - 12g | Potassium - 293.75mg | Cholesterol – 0mg | Sugar – 2g | Sodium – 329mg | Fiber – 23.2g

# 8   SALADS

## 8.1   Green Walnut Salad

Preparation Time: 10 minutes | Cooking Time: 0 minutes | Serving: 1

**Ingredients:**

- Cucumber – 3
- Olive oil – 1 ½ tbsp. (22.5ml)
- Lettuce (shredded) – 8 cups (450g)
- Walnuts – $^3/_8$ cup (45g)
- Salt – 1 ½ pinch (1.1g)
- Pepper – 1 ½ pinch (0.2g)

**Method:**

1. Fill the dish with lettuce. Cucumbers are peeled, sliced, and added.
2. Add the olive oil, salt, and pepper, and combine.
3. Smash walnuts, then add. Serve right away and delight in!

**Nutrition per serving:** Calories – 507 | Fat - 46g | Carbs - 19g | Protein - 13g | Potassium - 1235mg | Cholesterol – 0mg | Sugar – 6g | Sodium – 785mg | Fiber – 11g

## 8.2   Avocado Kale Salad

Preparation Time: 8 minutes | Cooking Time: 0 minutes | Serving: 1

**Ingredients:**

- Avocado – 2 (sliced)
- Kale – 4 (chopped)
- Pepper – ¼ tsp (0.5g)
- Salt – ¼ tsp (1.5g)
- Lemon juice – 4 tbsp. (60ml)

**Method:**

1. Cut the kale.
2. Mix greens and avocado. The kale will become more delicate as a result.
3. Add lime or lemon juice. Two tablespoons are roughly equal to one small or medium lemon.
4. Add pepper and salt to taste.
5. Toss again, then serve. Enjoy!

**Nutrition per serving:** Calories – 436 | Fat - 35g | Carbs - 25g | Protein - 7g | Potassium - 1437mg | Cholesterol – 0mg | Sugar – 2g | Sodium – 675mg | Fiber – 14g

## 8.3 Tofu Salad

Preparation Time: 10 minutes | Cooking Time: 0 minutes | Serving: 1

**Ingredients:**

- Lettuce – 2 cup (60g)
- Rocket leaves – 1 cup (23g)
- Tofu – 8 ounces (firm) (226.8g)
- Oregano – ¼ tbsp (0.75g)
- Salt – ¼ tbsp (3.7g)
- Lemon juice – 3 tbsp (45ml)

**Method:**

1. Crosswise, cut the tofu into four slabs.
2. Wipe as much wetness out as you can by alternating between layers of paper towels or clean tea towels.
3. Put in a single layer in the serving container you want to use to serve this.
4. Add the salt and oregano, and toss with the lemon juice and oil. Use after standing for 30 minutes as desired.
5. Add lettuce, rocket, tofu, oregano, salt and lemon juice in a bowl.
6. Toss all ingredients and serve.

**Nutrition per serving:** Calories – 256 | Fat - 16g | Carbs - 12g | Protein - 19.7g | Potassium - 722mg | Cholesterol – 0mg | Sugar – 2.5g | Sodium – 1505mg | Fiber – 5.6g

## 8.4 Corn and Black Bean Salad

Preparation Time: 25 minutes | Cooking Time: 0 minutes | Serving: 1

**Ingredients:**

- Red bell pepper – ¼ cup (37g)
- Corn – ¼ cup (41g)
- Onion – ¼ cup (40g)
- Black beans (boiled) – ½ cup (85g)
- Lemon juice – 3 tbsp (45ml)
- Salt and pepper – ¼ dash (0.016g)
- Olive oil – ¼ tbsp. (3.7ml)
- Cilantro – 2 tbsp. (6g)
- Pepper – ½ tbsp. (3g)

**Method:**

1. Drain and rinse the beans.
2. Chop the onion and bell pepper
3. Mix together all ingredients
4. Toss the spices and serve after allowing the flavors to mingle for at least 15 minutes.

**Nutrition per serving:**

Calories – 197 | Fat - 4.4g | Carbs - 34.7g | Protein - 8.5g | Potassium - 581mg | Cholesterol – 0mg | Sugar – 5.2g | Sodium – 210mg | Fiber – 9.5g

## 8.5   Kidney Bean Salad

Preparation Time: 10 minutes| Cooking Time: 0 minutes| Serving: 2

### Ingredients:

- Orange bell pepper – 1/3 cup (48g)
- Kidney beans – 1 1/3 cup (267g)
- Scallion – 1
- Parsley – 1 ½ cup (60g)
- Red pepper relish – 1/3 cup (76g)
- Celery stalk – 1/3
- Vinegar – 1 tsp (5ml)
- Olive oil – 2/3 tbsp (9.8ml)
- Salt and pepper – 1/3 dash (0.02g)

### Method:

1. Drain canned kidney beans, cut scallions, parsley, and red pepper before chopping celery.
2. In a medium bowl, combine all the ingredients and mix thoroughly
3. Taste and season as desired.

### Nutrition per serving:

Calories – 474| Fat - 12.5g | Carbs - 67.6g |Protein - 21.3g | Potassium - 1047mg | Cholesterol – 0mg |Sugar – 11.6g |Sodium – 545mg |Fiber – 20.6g

## 8.6   Tomato Spinach Salad

Preparation Time: 5 minutes| Cooking Time: 0 minutes| Serving: 1

### Ingredients:

- Medium tomato – 1 ½
- Scallions – 6 (medium)
- Spinach – 15 leaves (medium)
- Olive oil – 3 tbsp (45ml)
- Lemon – 1 ½ (medium)
- Pepper – 3

### Method:

1. After thoroughly washing the spinach, cut it. Squeeze out any extra water. Cut the tomato and scallions
2. Place the spinach in a mixing dish with the tomato, scallions, oil, pepper, and lemon juice. Toss and plate.

### Nutrition per serving:

Calories – 202| Fat - 18g | Carbs - 12g |Protein - 3g | Potassium - 705mg | Cholesterol – 0mg |Sugar – 5g |Sodium – 82mg |Fiber – 4g

## 8.7 Quinoa and Chickpea Salad

Preparation Time: 15 minutes| Cooking Time: 0 minutes| Serving: 3

### Ingredients:

- Cooked quinoa – 1 cup (185g)
- Boiled chickpeas – 1 cup (164g)
- Parsley – ¼ cup (15g)
- Lemon juice – ¼ cup (60ml)
- Fresh mint – ¼ cup (5g)
- Cucumber (diced) – ½ cup (60g)
- Cherry tomatoes – 1 cup (150g)
- Olive oil – 2tbsp (30ml)
- Salt and pepper – To Taste

### Method:

1. Combine all ingredients is a large bowl.
2. Add seasonings and olive oil.
3. Toss everything well and serve.

### Nutrition per serving:

Calories – 348| Fat - 12.2g | Carbs - 46.7g |Protein - 13.4g | Potassium - 622mg | Cholesterol – 0mg |Sugar – 5.7g |Sodium – 300mg |Fiber – 12.2g

## 8.8 Sweet Potato and Black Bean Salad

Preparation Time: 15 minutes| Cooking Time: 0 minutes| Serving: 1

### Ingredients:

- Boiled sweet potato – 2 (medium)
- Black beans – 1 can (14oz/400g)
- Onion – ½
- Cilantro (chopped) – ½ cup (8g)
- Red bell pepper – 1 (medium)
- Olive oil – 2 tbsp (30ml)
- Lemon juice – 2 tbsp (30ml)
- Salt and pepper – To Taste

### Method:

1. Take a large bowl, add all above ingredients.
2. Mix them well and serve
3. Bon appetite

### Nutrition per serving:

Calories – 449| Fat - 11g | Carbs - 78g |Protein - 17g | Potassium - 1427mg | Cholesterol – 0mg |Sugar – 13g |Sodium – 872mg |Fiber – 21g

## 8.9 Brussel Sprouts and Kale Salad

Preparation Time: 15 minutes | Cooking Time: 0 minutes | Serving: 1

**Ingredients:**

- Kale (chopped) – 4 cups (240g)
- Brussel sprouts (shaved) – 2 cups (300g)
- Parmesan cheese – ¼ cup (28g)
- Lemon juice – 2 tbsp (30ml)
- Olive oil – 2 tbsp (30ml)
- Salt and pepper – To Taste

**Method:**

1. Mix kale and Brussel sprouts.
2. Drizzle lemon juice, olive oil and salt and pepper.
3. Sprinkle grated parmesan cheese on top and enjoy.

**Nutrition per serving:**

Calories – 323| Fat - 23.4g | Carbs - 16.4g |Protein - 15.6g | Potassium - 988mg | Cholesterol – 22.3mg |Sugar – 3.5g |Sodium – 607mg |Fiber – 8.9g

## 8.10 Edamame and Tofu Salad

Preparation Time: 15 minutes | Cooking Time: 0 minutes | Serving: 4

**Ingredients:**

- Shelled edamame – 1 cup (150g)
- Firm tofu – 1 block (diced)
- Chopped cilantro – ¼ cup (4g)
- Chopped scallions – ½ cup (50g)
- Red bell pepper – 1 (diced)
- Rice vinegar – 2tbsp. (30ml)
- Sesame oil – 2 tbsp. (30ml)
- Salt and pepper – To Taste

**Method:**

1. Put all ingredients together.
2. Toss with all the seasonings.
3. Serve a power salad.

**Nutrition per serving:** Calories - 274| Fat - 17g | Carbs - 16g | Protein - 20g | Sugar - 4g | Potassium - 357mg | Cholesterol – 0mg |Sodium – 6mg |Fiber – 4g

## 8.11 Beet and Quinoa Salad

Preparation Time: 25 minutes | Cooking Time: 0 minutes | Serving: 2

**Ingredients:**

- Roasted beets – 2
- Cooked quinoa – 2 cups (420g)
- Goat cheese – ¼ cup (35g)
- Walnuts – ½ cup (60g)
- Olive oil – 2 tbsp. (30ml)
- Balsamic vinegar – 2tbsp. (30ml)
- Salt and pepper – To Taste

**Method:**

1. Roughly chop walnuts and crumble goat cheese.
2. Take a bowl, add all ingredients.
3. Add seasonings and serve.

**Nutrition per serving:**

Calories - 354| Fat - 20g | Carbs - 34g | Protein - 11g | Sugar - 8g | Potassium - 840mg | Cholesterol – 11mg |Sodium – 121mg |Fiber – 6g

## 8.12 Avocado and Mango Salad

Preparation Time: 15 minutes | Cooking Time: 0 minutes | Serving: 2

**Ingredients:**

- Avocadoes – 2 (diced)
- Mangoes – 2 (diced)
- Fresh cilantro – ¼ cup (4g)
- Olive oil – 2 tbsp. (30ml)
- Lime juice – 2 tbsp. (30ml)
- Salt and pepper – To Taste

**Method:**

1. Combine all ingredients in a bowl and mix them well.
2. Toss the salad and serve.

**Nutrition per serving:**

Calories - 301| Fat - 13g | Carbs - 45g | Protein - 9g | Sugar - 13g | Potassium - 543mg | Cholesterol – 0mg |Sodium – 7mg |Fiber – 11g

## 8.13 Caprese Salad

Preparation Time: 15 minutes| Cooking Time: 0 minutes| Serving: 1

### Ingredients:

- Large tomatoes – 2
- Fresh mozzarella – 8 oz. (227g)
- Fresh basil – ¼ cup (4g)
- Olive oil – 2 tbsp. (30ml)
- Balsamic vinegar – 2 tbsp. (30ml)
- Salt and pepper – To Taste

### Method:

1. Roughly chop tomatoes, basil and mozzarella.
2. Place them in a bowl and drizzle vinegar, olive oil, salt and pepper.
3. Serve your salad.

### Nutrition per serving:

Calories - 230| Fat - 17g | Carbs - 8g | Protein - 14g | Sugar - 5g | Potassium - 982mg | Cholesterol – 96mg | Sodium – 462mg |Fiber – 2g

## 8.14 Arugula and Fennel Salad

Preparation Time: 15 minutes| Cooking Time: 0 minutes| Serving: 1

### Ingredients:

- Bulb fennel – 1
- Arugula – 4 cups (120g)
- Parmesan – ¼ cup (25g)
- Olive oil – 2 tbsp. (30ml)
- Lemon juice – 2 tbsp. (30ml)
- Salt and pepper – To Taste

### Method:

1. Thinly slice fennel and them combine with arugula.
2. Pour all seasonings.
3. Top with shaved parmesan and serve.

### Nutrition per serving:

Calories - 140| Fat - 10g | Carbs - 9g | Protein - 6g | Sugar - 4g | Potassium - 1275mg | Cholesterol – 20mg |Sodium – 285mg |Fiber – 4g

## 8.15 Tuscan White Bean Salad

Preparation Time: 15 minutes | Cooking Time: 0 minutes | Serving: 1

**Ingredients:**

- Diced onion – ½ cup (90g)
- Cherry tomatoes – ½ cup (110g)
- Parsley – ½ cup (20g)
- White beans – 1 can (439g)
- Olive oil – 2tbsp. (30ml)
- Red wine vinegar – 2tbsp. (30ml)
- Salt and pepper – To Taste

**Method:**

1. Cut cherry tomatoes into 2 halves.
2. Combine all ingredients in a bowl and toss them.
3. Salad is ready to serve.

**Nutrition per serving:**

Calories - 214 | Fat - 8g | Carbs - 27g | Protein - 10g | Sugar - 1g | Potassium - 2104mg | Cholesterol – 0mg | Sodium – 947mg | Fiber – 8g

## 8.16 Potato Salad

Preparation Time: 15 minutes | Cooking Time: 5 minutes | Serving: 8

**Ingredients:**

- Potatoes – 5 (medium)
- Onion – 1 (medium)
- Celery stalk – 2 (medium)
- Vinegar – 3 tbsp. (45ml)
- Vegan mayo – 8 tbsp. (120ml)
- Salt and pepper – To Taste

**Method:**

1. Boil potatoes until they are almost tender (test with fork). Move to a strainer and chill.
2. Peel the potatoes if preferred when they have cooled, then slice them into bite-sized pieces.
3. Carefully combine all the ingredients in a large bowl and toss to combine. Season to taste with salt and pepper.

**Nutrition per serving:**

Calories - 200 | Fat - 9g | Carbs - 25g | Protein - 3g | Sugar - g | Potassium - 117mg | Cholesterol – 0mg | Sodium – 71mg | Fiber – 11g

# 9 BOWLS

## 9.1 Black Bean and Quinoa Bowl

Preparation Time: 10 minutes | Cooking Time: 20 minutes | Serving: 4

### Ingredients:

- Quinoa – 1 cup (185g)
- Rinsed black beans – 1 can (240g)
- Red bell pepper – 1 (diced)
- Red onion – 1 (diced)
- Avocado – 1 (diced)
- Olive oil – 2 tbsp. (30ml)
- Lemon juice – 2 tbsp. (30ml)
- Chili powder – 1 tbsp. (9g)
- Cumin – 1 tsp (8g)
- Fresh cilantro – ¼ cup (4g)
- Salt and pepper – To Taste

### Method:

1. Quinoa should be prepared as directed on the box.
2. Olive oil should be heated in a separate pan over medium heat. Red bell pepper and red onion should be added and sautéed for about 5 minutes, or until tender.
3. To the pan with the veggies, add the black beans as well as the cumin, chili powder, salt, and pepper. Cook for a further five minutes, stirring now and again.
4. Mix the lime juice and remaining olive oil in a small bowl.
5. Divide the cooked quinoa among the four bowls to construct the bowls. Add cilantro, chopped avocado, and the black bean and veggie combination to each bowl as garnish. Then mist the lime juice on top and serve.

### Nutrition per serving:

Calories - 420 | Fat - 20g | Carbs - 52g | Protein - 13g | Sugar - 2g | Potassium - 436mg | Cholesterol – 0mg | Sodium – 69mg | Fiber – 14g

## 9.2 Sweet Potato and Black Bean Bowl

Preparation Time: 10 minutes | Cooking Time: 25 minutes | Serving: 4

**Ingredients:**

- Cubed sweet potatoes – 2
- Drained black beans – 1 can (240g)
- Diced red bell pepper – 1
- Diced red onion – 1
- Diced avocado – 1
- Cumin – 1 tsp (8g)
- Chili powder – 1 tbsp. (9g)
- Olive oil – 2 tbsp. (30ml)
- Lemon juice – 2 tbsp. (30ml)
- Fresh cilantro – ¼ cup (4g)
- Salt and pepper – To Taste

**Method:**

1. Oven should be heated to 400°F (200°C).
2. On a baking sheet, distribute the cubed sweet potatoes and sprinkle with olive oil. Roast for 20 to 25 minutes in the oven, or until soft and gently browned.
3. Red bell pepper and red onion should be added and sautéed for about 5 minutes, or until tender.
4. Add remaining ingredients and cook for a further five minutes, stirring now and again.
5. Mix the lime juice and remaining olive oil in a small bowl.
6. Divide the cooked sweet potatoes among the four bowls to assemble the bowls. Add cilantro, chopped avocado, and the black bean and veggie combination to each bowl as garnish. Apply a lime glaze.

**Nutrition per serving:**

Calories - 420 | Fat - 20g | Carbs - 52g | Protein - 13g | Sugar - 2g | Potassium - 234mg | Cholesterol – 0mg | Sodium – 92mg | Fiber – 14g

## 9.3 Quinoa and Chickpea Bowl

Preparation Time: 5 minutes| Cooking Time: 0 minutes| Serving: 2

### Ingredients:

- Rinsed chickpeas – 1 can (240g)
- Cooked quinoa – 1 cup (185g)
- Diced cucumber – ½
- Diced red onion – ½
- Diced avocado – 1
- Lemon juice – 2 tbsp. (30ml)
- Olive oil – 2tbsp. (30ml)
- Chopped parsley – Garnishing
- Salt and pepper – To Taste

### Method:

1. Quinoa, chickpeas, cucumber, red onion, and avocado should all be combined in a bowl.
2. Add salt and pepper, drizzle with olive oil and lemon juice, and serve.
3. Add fresh parsley on top.

### Nutrition per serving:

Calories - 470| Fat - 28g | Carbs - 47g | Protein - 14g | Sugar - 1g | Potassium - 347mg | Cholesterol – 0mg |Sodium – 177mg |Fiber – 15g

## 9.4 Veg Tofu Bowl

Preparation Time: 5 minutes| Cooking Time: 5 minutes | Serving: 2

### Ingredients:

- Cooked rice – 1 cup (185g)
- Cubed tofu – ½ block
- Sliced zucchini – ½
- Sliced red bell pepper – ½
- Ginger powder – ½ tsp (1.5g)
- Soy sauce – 2 tbsp. (30ml)
- Sesame oil – 1 tbsp. (30ml)
- Sliced green onion – Garnishing
- Salt and pepper – To Taste

### Method:

1. For three to five minutes, sauté the tofu, red pepper and zucchini in a skillet with sesame oil.
2. Stir in the salt, pepper, soy sauce, ginger powder, and other seasonings.
3. Add chopped green onions on top before serving over cooked rice.

### Nutrition per serving:

Calories - 380| Fat - 10g | Carbs - 57g | Protein - 16g | Sugar - 1g | Potassium - 235mg | Cholesterol – 0mg |Sodium – 380mg |Fiber – 6g

## 9.5 Mediterranean Bowl

Preparation Time: 5 minutes | Cooking Time: 0 minutes | Serving: 2

**Ingredients:**

- Cooked quinoa – 1 cup (185g)
- Rinsed chickpeas – 1 can (429g)
- Diced cucumber – ½
- Diced red onion – ½
- Cherry tomatoes – ½ cup (halved) (110g)
- Kalamata olives – ¼ cup (90g)
- Dried oregano – 1 tsp (9g)
- Olive oil – 2 tbsp. (30ml)
- Red wine vinegar – 2 tbsp. (30ml)
- Chopped parsley – Garnishing
- Salt and pepper – To Taste

**Method:**

1. Quinoa, chickpeas, cucumber, red onion, cherry tomatoes, and olives should all be combined in a dish.
2. Add oregano, salt, and pepper, then drizzle with red wine vinegar and olive oil.
3. Add fresh parsley on top.

**Nutrition per serving:**

Calories - 400 | Fat - 18g | Carbs - 51g | Protein - 14g | Sugar - 3g | Potassium - 363mg | Cholesterol – 0mg | Sodium – 178mg | Fiber – 14g

## 9.6 Caprese Bowl

Preparation Time: 20 minutes | Cooking Time: 10 minutes | Serving: 2

**Ingredients:**

- Quinoa – 1 cup (185g)
- Vegetable broth – 2 cups (473ml)
- Diced avocado – 1
- Cherry tomatoes halved – 2 cups (220g)
- Diced fresh mozzarella – 8 ounces (227g)
- Chopped fresh basil – ¼ cup (4g)
- Balsamic vinegar – 2 tbsp. (30ml)
- Salt and pepper – To Taste

**Method:**

1. Quinoa should be rinsed before adding to a saucepan with vegetable broth. Bring to a boil, then lower the heat and simmer the quinoa for 15 to 20 minutes, or until it is ready.
2. Stir cooked quinoa, cherry tomatoes, avocado, mozzarella, and basil in a big bowl.
3. Add a dash of balsamic vinegar and flavor it with salt and pepper.

**Nutrition per serving:**

Calories - 412 | Fat - 20g | Carbs - 44g | Protein - 17g | Sugar - 2g | Potassium - 463mg | Cholesterol – 23mg | Sodium – 185mg | Fiber – 8g

## 9.7 Tuscan Bean and Vegetable Bowl

Preparation Time: 30 minutes | Cooking Time: 15 minutes | Serving: 2

### Ingredients:

- Rinsed cannellini beans – 1 can (429g)
- Chopped red onion – 1
- Sliced bell pepper – 1
- Sliced zucchini – 2
- Cherry tomatoes – 2 cups (220g)
- Olive oil – 2 tbsp. (30ml)
- Dried oregano – 1 tbsp. (4g)
- Salt and pepper – To Taste

### Method:

1. Oven should be heated to 400°F (200°C).
2. Cannellini beans, red onion, red peppers, zucchini, cherry tomatoes, olive oil, oregano, salt and pepper should all be combined in a big bowl.
3. Mixture should be spread out on a baking sheet, and veggies should be soft and gently browned after roasting for 25 to 30 minutes.
4. Serve plain or on a bed of quinoa or brown rice.

**Nutrition per serving:** Calories - 281 | Fat - 9g | Carbs - 40g | Protein - 12g | Sugar - 6g | Potassium - 605mg | Cholesterol – 0mg | Sodium – 231mg | Fiber – 13g

## 9.8 Parmesan Eggplant Bowl

Preparation Time: 25 minutes | Cooking Time: 20 minutes | Serving: 2

### Ingredients:

- Round sliced eggplant – 1
- Marinara sauce – 2 cups (473ml)
- Panko breadcrumbs – 1 cup (55g)
- Vegan mozzarella cheese – ½ cup (112g0
- Chopped basil – ¼ cup (4g)
- Italian seasonings – 2 tbsp. (30ml)
- Nutritional yeast – ½ cup (30g)
- Salt and pepper – To Taste

### Method:

1. Oven must be heated to 375°F (190°C).
2. Panko breadcrumbs, nutritional yeast, Italian seasoning, salt, and pepper should all be combined in a big basin.
3. Put the dipped eggplant rounds on a baking sheet covered with parchment paper after coating both sides with the breadcrumb mixture.
4. Round cuts of eggplant be baked for 20 to 25 minutes, or until soft and gently browned.
5. Sauce marinara is heated in a skillet over a medium flame.
6. Baked eggplant rounds, marinara sauce, vegan mozzarella cheese and fresh basil are all combined in a big dish.

7. Serve straight up over spaghetti.

**Nutrition per serving:**

Calories - 363| Fat - 19g | Carbs - 35g | Protein - 17g | Sugar - 15g | Potassium - 844mg | Cholesterol – 0mg |Sodium – 457mg |Fiber – 19g

## 9.9  Bibimbap Bowl

Preparation Time: 15 minutes| Cooking Time: 25 minutes| Serving: 2

**Ingredients:**

- Brown rice – 1 cup (202g)
- Carrot – 1
- Zucchini – 1
- Bean sprouts – 1 cup (184g)
- Spinach – 1 cup (30g)
- Kimchi – ½ cup (85g)
- Sliced tofu – ½ block
- Minced garlic – 1 clove
- Sesame oil – 1 tbsp. (15ml)
- Soy sauce – 1 tbsp. (15ml)
- Gochujang – 1 tbsp. (15ml)
- Rice vinegar – 1 tbsp. (15ml)
- Honey – 1 tbsp. (15ml)
- Salt and pepper – To Taste

**Method:**

1. According to the directions on the package, prepare the brown rice.
2. Make the veggies while the rice is cooking. Spinach, bean sprouts, carrots and zucchini should all be steam-cooked until soft but still little crunchy.
3. Mix the sesame oil, soy sauce, gochujang, rice vinegar, honey, garlic, salt, and pepper in a small bowl.
4. The tofu should be sautéed in a skillet until crisp and golden.
5. Place the rice at the bottom of the bowl, then the steamed veggies, the sautéed tofu, the kimchi, and finally the sauce.
6. Dispense and savor!

**Nutrition per serving:**

Calories - 541| Fat - 23g | Carbs - 70g | Protein - 17g | Sugar - 7g | Potassium - 477mg | Cholesterol – 0mg |Sodium – 308mg |Fiber – 9g

## 9.10 Japchae Bowl

Preparation Time: 15 minutes | Cooking Time: 20 minutes | Serving: 2

**Ingredients:**

- Sweet potato noodles – 4 ounces (120g)
- Carrot – 1
- Zucchini – 1
- Spinach – 1 cup (30g)
- Shiitake mushroom sliced – ½ cup (72.5g0
- Sliced onion – ½ cup (26g)
- Sliced tofu – ½ block
- Minced garlic – 1 clove
- Sesame oil – 2 tbsp. (30ml)
- Soy sauce – 1 tbsp. (15ml)
- Honey – 1 tbsp. (15ml)
- Rice vinegar – 1 tbsp. (15ml)
- Sesame seeds – Garnishing
- Sliced green onions – Garnishing
- Salt and pepper – To Taste

**Method:**

1. Follow the directions on the package to prepare the sweet potato noodles.
2. Make the veggies while the noodles are cooking. The carrot, zucchini and spinach should be steam-cooked until they are soft but still have a little firmness.
3. Sesame oil, soy sauce, honey, rice vinegar, garlic, salt, and pepper should all be combined in a small bowl.
4. The shiitake mushrooms and onion should be sautéed in a skillet until they are soft and caramelized. When the tofu is golden brown and crispy, add it and continue to cook.
5. Place the sweet potato noodles in the bottom of the dish, then the steamed veggies, the mushrooms, the tofu, and finally the sauce.
6. Sesame seeds and thinly sliced green onions are garnishes.
7. Dispense and savor!

**Nutrition per serving:**

Calories - 408 | Fat - 18g | Carbs - 57g | Protein - 14g | Sugar - 6g | Potassium - 393mg | Cholesterol – 0mg | Sodium – 477mg | Fiber – 5g

# 10 SOUPS AND STEWS

## 10.1 Potato and Carrot Stew

Preparation Time: 10 minutes| Cooking Time: 25 minutes| Serving:

**Ingredients:**

- Chopped onion – 1 ½ oz. (42.5g)
- Cubed carrots – 14 oz. (397g)
- Cubed potato – ½
- Curry powder – 2tbsp. (14g)
- Cooking spray – Spraying
- Vegetable broth – 3 cups (711ml)
- Coconut milk – ½ cup (118ml)
- Sal and pepper – To Taste

**Method:**

1. Place carrots, onion and potatoes in air fryer and spray cooking oil.
2. Bake them for 7 minutes on 350°F.
3. Transfer vegetables into food processor and make a smooth paste.
4. Add paste in a soup bowl and mix. Curry powder, coconut milk and vegetable stock. Season with pepper and salt.
5. Bring everything to boil for few minutes and serve hot.

**Nutrition per serving:**

Calories - 146| Fat – 7.4g | Carbs – 15.7g | Protein – 5.5g | Sugar – 6.9g | Potassium - 638mg | Cholesterol – 0mg | Fiber – 3.9 | Sodium – 638mg

## 10.2 Leak and Lentil soup

Preparation Time: 5 minutes| Cooking Time: 15 minutes| Serving: 3

**Ingredients:**

- Lentils – 3/8 cup (70g)
- Leeks – ¾ cup (55g)
- Vegetable broth – 3 3/8 cups (795ml)
- Large potato – 1
- Salt and pepper – To Taste

**Method:**

1. Cut the leek into thin slices after washing it thoroughly to remove any dirt (approx. 1cm). Put all the ingredients in a big pot.
2. Boil for two minutes, then lower the heat and simmer gently for about 20 minutes, stirring now and again.
3. Either in a blender or in the pan using a hand-held stick blender, season with salt and pepper to taste and mix until smooth. At this point, you may add a little extra water if you like a soup that is a bit thinner.

**Nutrition per serving:**

Calories - 569| Fat - 2g | Carbs - 110g |Protein - 31g |Sugar – 1.3g| Potassium - 278mg | Cholesterol – 0mg |Sodium – 195mg |Fiber – 4g

## 10.3 Arugula and Potato Soup

Preparation Time: 10 minutes | Cooking Time: 15 minutes | Serving: 4

### Ingredients:

- Arugula – 3 cups (90g)
- Potatoes – 4
- Onion – 1
- Garlic cloves – 3
- Olive oil – 1 tbsp. (15ml)
- Vegetable broth – 3 cups (710ml)
- Salt and pepper – To Taste

### Method:

1. Potato cubes, garlic cloves, and onion. Place the potatoes in a medium saucepan and add 2 inches of cold water. Give the water a lot of salt.
2. The potatoes should be cooked for 10 to 12 minutes, until they are soft, at a medium boil. Potatoes should be peeled after water has been drained.
3. In the same saucepan, heat the oil over medium heat. Sauté the onion and garlic until they begin to turn slightly brown. After adding the potatoes to the pan and cooking them for 3 to 5 minutes, add 2/3 of the stock.
4. When it begins to boil, add the rocket and cook it just until it begins to wilt. Add salt and pepper to taste. Remove from heat and allow it cool briefly.
5. Puree the potatoes and rocket in a blender until they are completely smooth. extra broth can be added to make liquid consistency. Ready to serve

### Nutrition per serving:

Calories - 745 | Fat - 15g | Carbs - 137g | Protein - 15g | Sugar - 2g | Potassium - 228mg | Cholesterol – 0mg | Sodium – 131mg | Fiber – 1g

## 10.4 Classic Tomato Soup

Preparation Time: 5 minutes | Cooking Time: 15 minutes | Serving: 2

### Ingredients:

- Canned tomatoes – 2 cups
- Garlic cloves – 2 (minced)
- Drained capers – 1 tbsp. (8g)
- Soy milk – ¾ cup (177ml)
- Olive oil – 1 tbsp. (15ml)

### Method:

1. Salt and pepper the garlic and capers as you lightly sauté them in oil in a sauce pan.
2. Add and mix the tomatoes.
3. Carefully purée the ingredients with a hand blender.
4. Add the soy milk, simmer, and continue mixing until desired smoothness is achieved.

### Nutrition per serving:

Calories - 362 | Fat - 18g | Carbs - 46g | Protein - 13g | Sugar - 6g | Potassium - 335mg | Cholesterol – 0mg | Sodium – 342mg | Fiber – 2.5g

## 10.5 Peanut Stew

Preparation Time: 10 minutes | Cooking Time: 30 minutes | Serving: 4

**Ingredients:**

- Tomatoes – 1 can (425g)
- Onion – 1
- Potato – 1
- Garlic – 1 tbsp. (8g)
- Chickpeas – 1 ½ cup (255g)
- Peanut butter – 1 cup (258g)
- Thyme leaves – 1/8 tbsp. (0.4g)
- Water – 1 cup (237ml)

**Method:**

1. Dice the potato, onion, and garlic.
2. In a medium saucepan, cook the onion until it is translucent and tender. then whisk in the garlic. After that, whisk in the tomatoes, peanut butter, and garbanzo beans. Add potato and season with thyme. Add 1-2 cups of water and whisk, depending on the desired thickness.
3. Put the lid on and cook for 25 to 35 minutes at low to medium heat. After the potatoes are fully cooked, the soup is finished. Enjoy!

**Nutrition per serving:** Calories – 547 | Fat - 34g | Carbs - 46g | Protein - 23g | Sugar - 4g | Potassium - 588mg | Cholesterol – 0mg | Sodium – 232mg | Fiber – 4g

## 10.6 Bean and Tomato Stew

Preparation Time: 5 minutes | Cooking Time: 20 minutes | Serving: 2

**Ingredients:**

- Tomato puree – 1 can (400g)
- Diced tomatoes – 1 cup (240g)
- Black beans – 1 can (240g)
- Chopped onion – 1
- Vegetable oil – 3 tbsp. (45ml)
- Salt – 1 tbsp. (18g)

**Method:**

1. Chop the onion, add to the heated oil in the pan, and cook until transparent.
2. Add tomato sauce and the diced tomato.
3. Bring to a boil, then lower the heat to a simmer, and let stew for approximately 20 minutes. At this point, add the can of beans. Add salt to the seafood and enjoy!

**Nutrition per serving:**
Calories - 873 | Fat - 44g | Carbs - 96g | Protein - 30g | Sugar - 6g | Potassium - 632mg | Cholesterol – 0mg | Sodium – 689mg | Fiber – 12g

## 10.7 Classic Lentil Soup

Preparation Time: 10 minutes | Cooking Time: 40 minutes | Serving: 4

### Ingredients:

- Dried lentils – 1 cup (200g)
- Bay leaf – 1
- Carrot – 1 (chopped)
- Celery stalk – 1 (chopped)
- Onion – 1 (chopped)
- Garlic cloves – 2 (minced)
- Vegetable broth – 4 cups (946ml)
- Olive oil – 1 tbsp. (15ml)
- Salt and pepper – To Taste

### Method:

1. Olive oil is heated over medium heat in a big saucepan.
2. Add the bay leaf, carrot, celery, onion, and garlic. With intermittently stirring, cook for 5 minutes.
3. Lentils should be soft after 30 to 40 minutes of simmering. Add lentils and stock, bring to a boil, then decrease heat.
4. To taste, add salt and pepper to the food.
5. Ready to serve!

**Nutrition per serving:** Calories - 217 | Fat - 4g | Carbs - 33g | Protein - 15g | Sugar - 2g | Potassium - 242mg | Cholesterol – 0mg | Sodium – 242mg | Fiber – 15g

## 10.8 Minestrone Soup

Preparation Time: 10 minutes | Cooking Time: 40 minutes | Serving: 4

### Ingredients:

- Carrot – 1 (chopped)
- Zucchini – 1 (chopped)
- Onion – 1 (chopped)
- Celery stalk – 2 (chopped)
- Garlic cloves – 2 (minced)
- Kidney bean – 1 can (450g)
- Diced tomatoes – 1 can (400g)
- Dried oregano – 1 tsp (8g)
- Dried basil – 1 tsp (8g)
- Olive oil – 1 tbsp. (15ml)
- Vegetable broth – 4 cups (946ml)
- Salt and pepper – To Taste

### Method:

1. Olive oil is heated over medium heat in a big saucepan. Add the zucchini, celery, carrot, onion and garlic.
2. Cook while stirring every 5-7 minutes. Basil, oregano, kidney beans, and vegetable broth should all be added.
3. When the veggies are soft, simmer for 20 to 30 minutes after bringing to a boil. To taste, add salt and pepper to the food.

**Nutrition per serving:** Calories - 191 | Fat - 4g | Carbs - 32g | Protein - 10g | Sugar - 2g | Potassium - 182mg | Cholesterol – 0mg | Sodium – 152mg | Fiber – 9g

## 10.9 Butternut Squash Soup

Preparation Time: 10 minutes | Cooking Time: 25 minutes | Serving: 4

**Ingredients:**

- Butternut squash – 1 (cubed)
- Onion – 1 (chopped)
- Garlic cloves – 2 (minced)
- Ground cinnamon – 1 tsp (8g)
- Ground nutmeg – ½ tsp (4g)
- Vegetable broth – 4 cups (946ml)
- Olive oil – 1 tbsp. (15ml)
- Salt and pepper – To Taste

**Method:**

1. Olive oil is heated over medium heat in a big saucepan. Cook for 2 to 3 minutes after adding the onion and garlic.
2. Add the veggie broth, nutmeg, cinnamon, and butternut squash. When the squash is ready, simmer for 20 to 25 minutes after bringing to a boil.
3. Once the soup is smooth, puree it in a blender or with an immersion blender.
4. To taste, add salt and pepper to the food and serve warm.

**Nutrition per serving:** Calories - 121 | Fat - 4g | Carbs - 23g | Protein - 2g | Sugar - 2g | Potassium - 279mg | Cholesterol – 0mg | Sodium – 145mg | Fiber – 4g

## 10.10 Creamy Cauliflower Soup

Preparation Time: 20 minutes | Cooking Time: 45 minutes | Serving: 5

**Ingredients:**

- Cauliflower head – 1 (chopped)
- Carrots – 3 (chopped)
- Chopped Onion – ½ cup (80g)
- Chopped Peeled yams – ½ lb. (227g)
- Chopped Potatoes – ½ lb. (227g)
- Red pepper – 1/8 tsp (0.3g)
- Salt – ½ tsp (2g)
- Grated ginger – 2 tsp (6g)
- Curry powder – 3 tsp (6g)
- Vegetable broth – 4 cups (946ml)
- Drained garbanzo – 15 ounces (242g)
- Unsweet soy milk – 14 ounces (415g)

**Method:**

1. Place the onions, beans, carrots, potatoes, sweet pepper, and cauliflower in a large soup pot over medium heat.
2. Add the vegetable stock to the soup pot after adding the salt, ginger, red pepper, and curry powder.
3. After 45 minutes of simmering on low heat, bring the entire liquid to a boil.
4. Add the soy milk and fully heat.
5. Present and savor.

**Nutrition per serving:** Calories - 398 | Fat - 3g | Carbs - 50g | Protein - 7g |

Sugar - 3g | Potassium - 237mg | Cholesterol – 0mg |Sodium – 122mg |Fiber – 2g

## 10.11 Gazpacho and Tomato Soup

Preparation Time: 15 minutes| Cooking Time: 0 minutes| Serving: 4

### Ingredients:

- Cucumber – 1 (chopped)
- Red onion – ½ (chopped)
- Red pepper – 1 (chopped)
- Tomato juice – 3 cups (711ml)
- Hot sauce – 3 tsp (15ml)
- Salt and pepper – To Taste

### Method:

1. Place everything in a food processor.
2. Whirl for one minute, first at a moderate speed and then at a fast speed.
3. Soup is ready and can be enjoyed warm or chilled.

### Nutrition per serving:

Calories - 153| Fat - 1g | Carbs - 12g | Protein - 2g | Sugar - 7g | Potassium - 500mg | Cholesterol – 0mg |Sodium – 383mg |Fiber – 3g

## 10.12 Vegetable and Farro Soup

Preparation Time: 20 minutes| Cooking Time: 30 minutes| Serving: 12

### Ingredients:

- Farro – 1 cup (200g)
- Vegetable stock – 1 box (907g)
- Diced tomatoes – 2 cans (822g)
- Chopped kale – 2 cups (130g)
- Cannellini beans – 2 cans (878g)
- Chopped carrots – 3
- Sliced leeks – 2 inches
- Minced garlic cloves – 4
- Chopped celery stalk – 4
- Chopped onion – 1
- Chopped potatoes – 1 ½ cups (200g)
- Sliced Napa cabbage – 1 bunch
- Sweet corn – 2 cans (864g)
- Dried tarragon – 1 ½ tsp (1.5g)
- Dried coriander – 1 tsp (2g)
- Fresh thyme – 1 tbsp. (6g)
- Turmeric – ½ tsp (1g)
- Salt and pepper – To Taste

### Method:

1. Add the leeks, onion, garlic, celery, carrots, and potatoes to a large soup pot and sauté with 1/4 cup vegetable stock.
2. Add the salt and pepper and toss intermittently until the onions are transparent.
3. Add the other ingredients and spices, cover, and simmer for 30 minutes on low heat

4. Present and savor.

**Nutrition per serving:** Calories - 212 | Fat - 2g | Carbs - 41g | Protein - 10g | Sugar -6 g | Potassium - 593mg | Cholesterol – 0mg | Sodium – 868mg | Fiber – 9g

## 10.13 Coconut Yam Soup

Preparation Time: 20 minutes | Cooking Time: 50 minutes | Serving: 6

**Ingredients:**

- Rinsed garbanzo beans – 1 can (240g)
- Cubed sweet potato – 1 large
- Red lentils – ½ cup (90g)
- Minced garlic – 3 cloves
- Crushed tomatoes – 14 ounces (397g)
- Vegetable broth – 4 cups (946ml)
- Soy milk – 2 cups (473ml)
- Coconut extract – 2 tsp (10ml)
- Almond butter – 2 tbsp. (30ml)
- Maple syrup – 1 ½ tbsp. (23ml0
- Minced ginger – 1 tbsp. (6g)
- Garam masala – 1 tsp (2g)
- Cumin – 1 tsp (2g)
- Cinnamon – ¼ tsp (0.5g)
- Curry powder – 1 ½ tsp (3g)

**Method:**

1. Place all the ingredients in a large soup pot and bring to a boil.
2. Lower the heat, cover, and simmer for 45 minutes.
3. Dish out and savor.

**Nutrition per serving:** Calories - 326 | Fat - 7g | Carbs - 51g | Protein - 15g | Sugar - 10g | Potassium - 1045mg | Cholesterol – 0mg | Sodium – 888mg | Fiber – 14g

## 10.14 Mushroom Stew

Preparation Time: 20 minutes | Cooking Time: 20 minutes | Serving: 6

**Ingredients:**

- Tomato paste – 6 ounces (170g)
- Chopped mushrooms – 16 ounces (453g)
- Sliced yellow onion – 1
- Chopped carrots – 3
- Celery stalk chopped – 3
- Thawed frozen peas – 2 cups (356g)
- Chopped potatoes – 2 lb. (907g)
- Minced garlic – 6 cloves
- Tamari 3 tbsp. (44g)
- Water – 3 cups (710ml)
- Smoked paprika – ½ tbsp. (3g)
- Fresh rosemary – 1 tbsp. (2g)
- Italian herbs – 1 tbsp. (2g)
- Vegetable stock – 2 cups (473ml)
- Salt and pepper – To Taste

**Method:**

1. In a large soup pot, add 1/4 cup of water, the onion, celery, and carrots, and sauté until they are soft. Then, add the mushroom and garlic, and continue to sauté for a few minutes longer.

2. Fill the soup pot with the following ingredients: salt, water, herbs, pepper, tamari, potatoes, tomato paste, smoked paprika, and vegetable stock. Cook, covered, over medium heat, until the vegetables are fork-tender.

3. Transfer 2 cups of the vegetables and broth to a food processor, and pulse until smooth.

4. Re-pour the sauce into the saucepan and whisk to mix.

5. Add the frozen peas and cook for 5 minutes more.

6. Serve with crusty garlic bread as a side.

**Nutrition per serving:**

Calories - 202 | Fat - 2g | Carbs - 43g | Protein - 7g | Sugar - 8g | Potassium - 792mg | Cholesterol – 0mg |Sodium – 120mg |Fiber – 9g

## 10.15 Veg Soup with Ravioli

Preparation Time: 30 minutes| Cooking Time: 20 minutes| Serving: 6

**Ingredients:**

- Cannellini beans – 1 cup (180g)
- Chopped onions – 1 cup (160g)
- Chopped carrots – 1 cup (128g)
- Chopped bell peppers – 1 cup (120g)
- Crushed can tomatoes – 16 ounces (453g)
- Chopped kale – 6 stems
- Diced zucchini – 2
- Fresh ravioli – 1 package
- Minced garlic – 2 cloves
- Red pepper – ¼ tsp (0.5g)
- Dried basil – 1 tsp (1g)
- Vegetable stock – 6 cups (1419ml)
- Salt and pepper – To Taste

**Method:**

1. In a large soup pot, combine the onions, carrots, and peppers with 2 tablespoons water. Cook for a few minutes, stirring periodically.

2. Add the red pepper and garlic and heat for an additional minute.

3. Add the kale, beans, tomatoes, basil, zucchini and vegetable stock. Boil over high heat.

4. Add salt and pepper to the soup.

5. Prepare the ravioli in a separate pan in accordance with the directions on the package.

6. Dish out the ravioli and soup separately and savor.

**Nutrition per serving:**

Calories - 315| Fat - 4g | Carbs - 59g | Protein - 16g | Sugar - 9g | Potassium - 190mg | Cholesterol – 0mg |Sodium – 200mg |Fiber – 14g

## 10.16 Italian Pasta Stew

Preparation Time: 25 minutes| Cooking Time: 35 minutes| Serving: 4

**Ingredients:**

- Chopped carrots – 2
- Chopped celery stalk – 2
- Chopped red bell pepper – 1
- Chopped onion – 1
- Rinsed chickpeas – 1 can (425g)
- Drained cannellini beans – 1 can (425g)
- Diced tomatoes – 1 can (396g)
- Small pasta – ½ cup (56g)
- Chopped parsley – ½ cup (8g)
- Minced garlic – 3 cloves
- Dried oregano – 1 tsp (1g)
- Dried basil – 1 tsp (1g)
- Dried thyme – ½ tsp (0.5g)
- Vegetable broth – 2 cups (473g)
- Salt and pepper – To Taste

**Method:**

1. Cook the red bell pepper, carrots, and celery for a further five minutes, or until the veggies begin to soften.

2. Add salt, pepper, oregano, basil, thyme, vegetable broth, chickpeas, and cannellini beans

3. after dicing the tomatoes. For 20 to 25 minutes, or until the veggies are cooked, bring the mixture to a simmer.

4. Add the pasta to cook for another 10 minutes until pasta is soft and serve the stew hot with chopped parsley as a garnish.

**Nutrition per serving:** Calories - 503| Fat - 5g | Carbs - 53g | Protein - 15g | Sugar - 2g | Potassium - 247mg | Cholesterol – 0mg |Sodium – 178mg |Fiber – 11g

# 11 PASTA, RICE & GRAINS

## 11.1 Spinach & Lentil Rice

Preparation Time - 2 minutes | Cooking Time - 12 minutes | Serves 1

### Ingredients:

- White rice – 4 tbsp (28.35g)
- Spinach (boiled) – 3 tbsp (22g)
- Yellow lentils (dry) – 2 tbsp. (16g)
- Onions (chopped) – 1 tbsp. (10g)
- Garlic powder – 1 tsp (3g)
- Salt – 2 tsp (10g)
- Red pepper – 2 tsp (4g)
- Butter – 1 tsp (5g)
- Cinnamon – ¼ tsp (0.6g)

### Method:

1. Boil rice and lentils together until rice is softened
2. In a pan, add butter and saute onions, add spices and spinach and let it simmer for 2 minutes
3. Add boiled rice and lentils, cover the lid for 2 minutes
4. Serve with Hash browns

**Nutrition per serving:** Calories - 251 | Fat 2.9g | Carbs 48.2g | Protein 9.5g | Sugar 1.8g | Potassium 387.5mg | Cholesterol – 8mg | Sodium – 1437mg | Fiber – 3.3g

## 11.2 Creamy Mushroom Pasta

Preparation Time - 2 minutes | Cooking Time - 15 minutes | Serves 2

### Ingredients:

- Fettuccine Pasta (boiled) – 1 cup (120g)
- White or brown mushrooms – 2 cup (180g)
- Garlic paste – 1 tbsp. (15g)
- Onions – 1 large
- Salt – according to taste
- Paprika powder – 2 tsp (4g)
- Black pepper – 1 tbsp. (6g)
- Vegetable oil – 2 tbsp. (30ml)
- Vegetable broth – 1½ cup (355ml)
- Soy sauce – 1 tbsp. (15ml)
- Parsley – ½ bunch
- All purpose flour – 2 tbsp. (16g)
- Cream – ¾ cup (177ml)
- Basil leaves (crushed) – 1 tsp (0.5g)

### Method:

1. Clean the mushrooms and cut in thin slices
2. Heat oil in a pan and saute onions, add garlic and mushrooms
3. Dust with flour, add spices and sauce and let it sweat
4. Add cream and let it simmer for 3-5 minutes, on low flame
5. In a pasta plate, spread pasta, drizzle over the creamy mushrooms
6. Garnish with parsley and basil leaves

**Nutrition per serving:** Calories - 654| Fat 38.9g| Carbs 59.7g| Protein 14.2g| Sugar 7.8g| Potassium 666mg | Cholesterol – 109mg |Sodium – 1545mg |Fiber – 4.8g

## 11.3 Vegetable Lasagna

Preparation Time - 5 minutes| Cooking Time - 30 minutes| Serves 2

### Ingredients:

- Lasagna strips (boiled) – 5-7
- Spinach – 1 cup (30g)
- Potatoes (sliced) – 4 medium sized
- Red bell pepper – 1 medium sized
- Onion – 1 medium sized
- Olive oil – 2 tsp (10ml)
- Cheese – 6 oz (170g)
- Garlic powder 1 tbsp. (9g)
- Black pepper – 1 tbsp. (6g)
- Salt – according to taste
- Paprika powder – 2 tsp (4g)

### For bechamel sauce:

- Almond milk – 2 ¾ cup (650ml)
- Butter – 1 ½ tbsp. (21g)
- All-purpose flour – 2 tbsp. (16g)
- Salt – 1 tsp (5.7g)
- Nutmeg – 1 tsp (2.5g)
- Pepper – 2 tsp (4g)

### Method:

1. Boil potatoes until soft
2. Heat oil in a pan, saute onions add garlic powder and stir for a min
3. Add bell pepper and spices and let it simmer for another min
4. Add spinach let it sit until water dries, and spinach is mixed
5. For sauce, melt the butter in a pan add flour and let it sweat for a minute
6. Add milk and season with spices
7. Toss potato slices in a microwave bowl and spinach mixture on top of it
8. Layer it with sauce and lasagna
9. Top it with grated cheese and microwave for 5 minutes

**Nutrition per serving:** Calories - 719| Fat 36.6g| Carbs 71.9g| Protein 27.8g| Sugar 14.5g| Potassium 445.5mg | Cholesterol – 1636mg |Sodium – 1216mg |Fiber – 10.2g

## 11.4 Vegan Mushroom Risotto

Preparation Time - 10 minutes | Cooking Time - 30-40 minutes | Serves 3

### Ingredients:

- Mushrooms – 16 oz (454g)
- Olive oil – 2 tbsp. (30ml)
- Onion (chopped) – 1 medium sized
- Garlic (grated) – 3 cloves
- Black pepper – according to taste or 1 ½ tbsp. (11.25g)
- Salt – according to taste
- Risotto rice (arborio) – 1 cup (190g)
- Vegan butter – 2 tbsp. (28g)
- Vegetable stock – 4 cups (960ml)
- White wine – ¼ cup (60g)

### Method:

1. Add oil to a pot and saute onions on medium flame until softened
2. Toss garlic and sliced mushrooms into the pot
3. Cover the lid and let the mushrooms simmer until softened
4. Add risotto rice and saute
5. Add a little more than half of vegetable stock, stir well and let it simmer by covering the lid until almost all water is absorbed
6. Add the leftover vegetable stock, stir and let it absorb
7. When all stock is absorbed, add vegan butter and remove from flame cover the lid for another minute
8. Serve hot!

**Nutrition per serving:** Calories - 447| Fat 11g| Carbs 74g| Protein 9g| Sugar 5g| Potassium 346mg | Cholesterol – 0mg |Sodium – 1262mg |Fiber – 4g

## 11.5 Vegetable Fried Rice

Preparation Time - 10 minutes | Cooking Time - 30 minutes | Serves 4

### Ingredients:

- Rice – 2 cups (360g)
- Water – as required
- Vegetable broth – 1 cup (240ml)
- Onion (chopped) – 1 medium sized
- Garlic (minced) – 2 cloves
- Carrot (chopped) – 1 medium sized
- Bell pepper (chopped) – 1 medium sized
- Peas – 1 cup (160g)
- Salt – to taste
- Pepper – to taste
- Vegetable oil – 2 tbsp. (30ml)
- Sesame oil – 1 tbsp. (15ml)
- Soy sauce – 2 tbsp. (30ml)

### Method:

1. In a pot, heat vegetable oil cook onions until light brown
2. Add garlic and stir
3. Add spices and sauces, add peas and cook for 2 minutes
4. Add bell pepper and carrots, cook for around 5 minutes with splashes of vegetable stock, while stirring
5. Add 2 cups water and bring it to boil
6. Add rice and wait until almost all water is absorbed

7. Check if the rice is softened, if not add little more water and let it absorb
8. Cover the lid, and place the pot on very low flame for 5 minutes
9. Serve hot!

**Nutrition per serving:** Calories - 348| Fat 7g| Carbs 62g| Protein 7g| Sugar 5g| Potassium 445.5mg | Cholesterol – 0mg |Sodium – 648mg |Fiber – 5g

## 11.6 Mushroom & Vegetable Wild Rice Pilaf

Preparation Time - 10 minutes| Cooking Time - 30 minutes| Serves 2

### Ingredients:

- Rice – 1 cup (180g)
- Vegetable broth – 2 cup (480g)
- Mushrooms – 8 oz (240g)
- Onion (chopped) – 1 medium sized
- Garlic (chopped) – 2 cloves
- Dried thyme – 1 tsp (1.5g)
- Pepper – to taste
- Salt – to taste
- White Sesame seeds – a large pinch (0.5g)
- Olive oil – 1 tbsp. (15ml)
- Parsley (fresh) – 2 tbsp. (8g)

### Method:

1. Heat onions with oil until translucent, add garlic and saute
2. Add mushrooms with spices and thyme until they release the moisture
3. Add vegetable broth, bring to boil and add rice, turn the flame to medium low
4. Once all water is absorbed, turn the flame to very low, cover the lid and let it sit for 5 minutes
5. Add parsley, sprinkle the sesame seeds and serve hot!

**Nutrition per serving:** Calories - 299| Fat 7.8g| Carbs 50.7g| Protein 7.3g| Sugar 3.8g| Potassium 439mg | Cholesterol – 0mg |Sodium – 492mg |Fiber – 3.6g

## 11.7 Lentil & Vegetable Salad with Brown Rice

Preparation Time - 10 minutes | Cooking Time - 40 minutes | Serves 3

### Ingredients:

- Brown rice – 1 cup (240g)
- Green lentils – ½ cup (120g)
- Pepper – to taste
- Salt – to taste
- Yellow bell pepper (chopped) – 1 medium sized
- Red bell pepper (chopped) – 1 medium sized
- Carrots (shredded) – 1 medium sized
- Fresh parsley – ½ cup (30g)
- Red onions (chopped) – 1 medium sized
- Balsamic vinegar – 2 tbsp. (30ml)
- Vegetable oil – 2 tsp (10ml)
- Olive oil – 1 tbsp. (15ml)

### Method:

1. Boil rice
2. In a pot heat vegetable oil and saute onions, add garlic and saute
3. Add spices and bell peppers, cook on low flame for 2 minutes
4. Add lentils and vegetable stock, turn the flame to medium and cover the lid
5. Let it simmer for 5 minutes or until all water is absorbed
6. Pour the mixture into a bowl with rice, add shredded carrots, olive oil and balsamic vinegar
7. Add more spices if desired, and shred parsley over

**Nutrition per serving:** Calories - 374| Fat 8g| Carbs 64g| Protein 13g| Sugar 6g| Potassium 726mg | Cholesterol – 0mg |Sodium – 341mg |Fiber – 14g

## 11.8 Vegetable Quinoa Fried Rice

Preparation Time - 10 minutes | Cooking Time - 20 minutes | Serves 2

### Ingredients:

- Quinoa (boiled) – ½ cup (93g)
- Onions (chopped) – 2 tbsp. (20g)
- Scallions (chopped) – 2 tbsp. (10g)
- Garlic (minced) – 2 cloves
- Carrot (chopped) – 1 medium sized
- Broccoli (diced) – 2 cup (150g)
- Bell pepper (chopped) – 1 medium sized
- Peas – ½ cup (70g)
- Roasted Cashew nut – 1 oz (28g)
- Lemon juice – 2 tbsp. (30ml)
- Sesame oil – 1 tbsp. (15ml)

### Method:

1. Add chopped onions to a pot and saute in with oil, add vegetables and heat until tender
2. Add spices, cashew nuts and lemon juice. Stir well
3. Add quinoa and stir-fry until crispy
4. Serve hot!

**Nutrition per serving:** Calories - 342| Fat 12g| Carbs 49g| Protein 12g| Sugar 8g| Potassium 877mg | Cholesterol – 0mg |Sodium – 186mg |Fiber – 11g

## 11.9 Vegetable Spaghetti Bolognese

Preparation Time - 10 minutes | Cooking Time - 30-35 minutes | Serves 2

### Ingredients:

- Spaghetti (boiled) – 1 cup (100g)
- Tomato puree – 2 tbsp. (30ml)
- Tomatoes (chopped) – 4 medium sized
- Onions (chopped) – 1 medium sized
- Carrots (chopped) – ¾ cup (75g)
- Garlic cloves (grated) – 2
- Olive oil – 1 tbsp. (15ml)
- Oregano – 1 tsp (1.8g)
- Basil leaves (dry) – 1 tsp (0.8g)
- Balsamic vinegar – 1 tbsp. (15ml)
- Mushrooms (diced) – ¾ cup (75g)
- Almond milk – 3 tbsp. (45ml)
- Soy sauce – 2 tbsp. (30ml)
- Salt – to taste

### Method:

1. In a pan heat oil, add onions, garlic and carrots and cook until softened
2. Stir in tomato puree, vinegar and oregano, then add mushrooms and tomatoes
3. Reduce heat, let it simmer until the sauce thickens as desired, splash water if it catches the bottom of pan
4. Stir the soy sauce and milk
5. Place spaghetti in a pasta plate and spread the vegetable curry over garnish with basil leaves

**Nutrition per serving:** Calories - 385 | Fat 10g | Carbs 68g | Protein 12g | Sugar 16g | Potassium 1267mg | Cholesterol – 0mg | Sodium – 490mg | Fiber – 12g

## 11.10 Vegetable Fettuccine Alfredo

Preparation Time - 10 minutes | Cooking Time - 20 minutes | Serves 2

### Ingredients:

- Fettuccine noodles (boiled) – 8 oz (227g)
- Garlic cloves – 4
- Onion powder – ½ tsp (1.5g)
- Olive oil – 2 tbsp. (30ml)
- Vegetable broth – 2 cup (473ml)
- Cashew nuts – ½ cup (64g)
- Almond milk – ½ cup (118ml)
- All purpose flour – 2 tbsp. (16g)
- Nutmeg – pinch (0.2)
- Kosher salt – to taste
- Black pepper – to taste
- Basil leaves (dry)– 1 tsp (0.8g)
- Fresh parsley – 1 tbsp. (3g)

### Method:

1. Heat oil in a large pot, add cashews and saute until light brown
2. Add garlic and saute, add flour mix well
3. Add milk and spices and let it simmer
4. Remove from heat when desired thickness appears
5. Add fettuccine to the sauce
6. Serve with fresh parsley and basil leaves on top

**Nutrition per serving:** Calories - 623| Fat 26.3g| Carbs 80.2g| Protein 20.5g| Sugar 5.9g| Potassium 657.7mg | Cholesterol – 0mg |Sodium – 727.5mg |Fiber – 7.4g

## 11.11 Pesto Pasta with Spinach and Cherry tomatoes

Preparation Time - 2 minutes| Cooking Time - 12 minutes| Serves 1

### Ingredients:

- Penne pasta (boiled) – 8 oz (227g)
- Basil pesto – ½ cup (120g)
- Baby spinach (wilted) – 8 oz (227g)
- Cherry tomatoes – 5-7 halved
- Salt – to taste
- Black pepper – to taste
- Lemon juice – 1 tbsp. (15ml)
- Basil leaves – 2 tsp (1g)

### Method:

1. Add pasta and spinach to a bowl
2. Add in pesto, stir well
3. Toss in tomatoes, salt and pepper
4. Add lemon juice, sprinkle basil leaves and Serve hot!

**Nutrition per serving:** Calories - 673| Fat 38g| Carbs 68g| Protein 18g| Sugar 6g| Potassium 543mg| Cholesterol – 18mg |Sodium – 962mg |Fiber – 7g

## 11.12 Vegetable Mushroom Stroganoff

Preparation Time - 5 minutes| Cooking Time - 30 minutes| Serves 2

### Ingredients:

- Noodles – 7 oz (200g)
- Onion (chopped) – 1 cup (150g)
- Mushrooms (sliced) – 8 oz (227g)
- Thyme leaves (fresh) – 1 tbsp. (3g)
- Garlic – 3 cloves
- All purpose flour – 3 tbsp. (23g)
- Sea salt – to taste
- Pepper – to taste
- Vegetable broth – 3 cup (710ml)
- Almond milk – ½ cup (120ml)
- Parmesan cheese – as required

### Method:

1. Heat oil in a pot, add onions and saute, then add mushrooms and heat until golden and all all water released is absorbed
2. Add garlic and thyme and cook until garlic is fragrant
3. Add flour and mix, add spices
4. Add vegetable stock while stirring to avoid lumps
5. Add noodles and let them dip completely into the stock
6. Let it simmer, then add milk
7. Stir gently to avoid breaking noodles
8. Cook until desired thickness appears
9. Garnish with parsley and cheese and serve while hot!

**Nutrition per serving:** Calories - 499| Fat 10g| Carbs 86g| Protein 17g| Sugar 10g| Potassium 1043mg | Cholesterol – 16.3mg |Sodium – 780mg |Fiber – 10g

## 11.13 Vegan One-Pot Pasta

Preparation Time - 5 minutes| Cooking Time - 25 minutes| Serves 2

Ingredients:

- Olive oil – 2 tsp (10ml)
- Garlic – 2 cloves
- Onions – ½ medium sized
- Mushrooms – 1 ½ cup (150g)
- Non-dairy milk – 1½ cup (355ml)
- Vegetable broth – 2 cup (473ml)
- Pasta (of choice) – 7 oz (200g)
- Corn starch – 2 tsp (6g)
- Water – as required
- Pepper – 1 tsp (2g)
- Salt – to taste
- Vegan butter – 2 tsp (9.2g)
- Basil – 2 tbsp. (8g)

Method:

1. Saute onion and garlic in olive oil
2. Add mushrooms and saute for 5 minutes
3. Add milk and broth, bring it to boil
4. Add pasta and bring it to boil, and add water if required
5. While cooking pasta, add cornstarch to 1 tbsp. water and stir
6. Add spices, cornstarch slurry and butter to the pasta
7. Turn off the heat
8. Serve in pasta platter and garnish with basil

**Nutrition per serving:** Calories - 455| Fat 11g| Carbs 76g| Protein 16g| Sugar

8g| Potassium 526mg | Cholesterol – 0mg |Sodium – 742mg |Fiber – 7g

## 11.14 Seeds & Oats Porridge

Preparation Time - 5 minutes| Cooking Time - 12 minutes| Serves 2

Ingredients:

- Pumpkin seeds – 1 tbsp. (7g)
- Chia seeds – 1 tbsp. (9g)
- Flaxseeds – 1 tbsp. (10g)
- Sunflower seeds – 1 tbsp. (6g)
- Raisins – 1 tbsp. (14g)
- Oats bran – 2 tbsp. (13g)
- Steel cut oats – 1 tbsp. (6g)
- Walnuts (chopped) – 2 tbsp. (14g)
- Almond milk – 2 cup (473ml)
- Dates (chopped) – 4
- Bananas & Raspberries (chopped) – as preferred

Method:

1. Boil almond milk, add seeds, grains and oats, let it simmer until lentils become soft
2. Add nuts and dry fruits, let it simmer
3. Top with fruits
4. Serve & enjoy!

**Nutrition per serving:** Calories - 758| Fat 23.5g| Carbs 118g| Protein 26.9g| Sugar 24.7g| Potassium 742.5mg | Cholesterol – 0mg |Sodium – 16mg |Fiber – 10g

## 11.15 Roasted Vegetable & Quinoa Combo

Preparation Time - 10 minutes| Cooking Time - 40 - 50 minutes| Serves 2

## Ingredients:

- Quinoa – 1 cup (185g)
- Olive oil – 1 tbsp. (15ml)
- Zucchini (sliced) – 1 medium sized
- Sweet potato (sliced to 1 inch chunks) – 1 medium sized
- Onions (chopped) – 1 medium sized
- Red bell pepper (chopped) – 1 medium sized
- Yellow bell pepper (chopped) – 1 medium sized
- Kale (chopped) – 2 cup (130g)
- Smoked paprika – 1 tsp (2g)
- Salt – to taste
- Pepper – to taste

### For dressing

- Lemon juice – 3 tbsp. (45ml)
- Tahini – ⅓ cup (76g)
- Garlic clove – 2

## Method:

1. Place all vegetables except kale on oven trays evenly, toss with salt and pepper and drizzle over olive oil, toss again to spread evenly
2. Roast the veggies for 20-40 minutes as preferred, change sides in between to prevent burning one side
3. In a pan, add water quinoa and pinch of salt, bring to boil and let it simmer until it fluffs
4. Combine all ingredients for dressing and mix
5. In a large bowl, layer half quinoa, half veggies and kale
6. Drizzle a layer of dressing
7. Repeat the process with second layer
8. Serve and enjoy!

## Nutrition per serving:

Calories - 540| Fat 16g| Carbs 85g| Protein 17g| Sugar 11g| Potassium 1381.4mg | Cholesterol – 0mg |Sodium – 387mg |Fiber – 16g

## 11.16 Brown Rice & Lentil Casserole

Preparation Time - 5 minutes | Cooking Time - 30 minutes | Serves 2

### Ingredients:

- Brown rice – ½ cup (100g)
- Lentils – ¾ cup (150g)
- Vegetable stock – 3 cups (710ml)
- Onion (chopped) – ¾ cup (90g)
- Cheese (grated) – 8 oz (226g)
- Garlic powder – ¼ tsp (0.5g)
- Italian seasoning – 1 tsp (1.5g)
- Salt & pepper – to taste

### Method:

1. Preheat the oven to 300°C (572°F)
2. Add all ingredients except cheese to a baking tray and bake for around 20 minutes
3. Add cheese and bake for another 10 minutes
4. Serve hot!

### Nutrition per serving:

Calories - 430 | Fat 23g | Carbs 21.7g | Protein 35.7g | Sugar 4.7g | Potassium 230mg | Cholesterol – 0mg | Sodium – 104mg | Fiber – 5.7g

## 11.17 Black Bean Chili Quinoa

Preparation Time - 5 minutes | Cooking Time - 15 minutes | Serves 3

### Ingredients:

- Quinoa – ½ cup (93g)
- Onion – 1 medium sized
- Garlic – 2 cloves
- Tomatoes – 1 ⅔ cup (250g)
- Vegetable stock – 2 ½ cup (590ml)
- Avocados (sliced) – 1 small
- Black beans – 1 ⅔ cup (330g)
- Olive oil – 2 tsp (10ml)
- Hot paprika powder – 1 tsp (2g)
- Cumin powder – 2 tsp (6g)
- Red chili (chopped) – 1
- Coriander leaves – few

### Method:

1. Fry onion, garlic and red chili in olive oil, then add spices
2. Add quinoa, tomatoes, black beans, stock and Season well
3. Cover it until quinoa is tender
4. Top it with avocado slices and coriander leaves to serve

**Nutrition per serving:** Calories - 388 | Fat 14g | Carbs 54g | Protein 15g | Sugar 5.6g | Potassium 1216mg | Cholesterol – 0mg | Sodium – 185mg | Fiber – 6.2g

## 11.18 Herbed Bulgur & Lentil Pilaf

Preparation Time - 30 minutes | Cooking Time - 60 minutes | Serves 4

### Ingredients:

- Bulgur – 1 cup (182g)
- Green lentils – ½ cup (90g)
- Vegetable broth – 4 cups (946ml)
- Olive oil – 2 tsp (10ml)
- Yellow bell pepper – 1 medium sized
- Onion – 1 medium sized
- Basil leaves – 2 tbsp. (7.6g)
- Parsley – 2 tbsp. (8g)
- Fresh chives – 2 tbsp. (8g)
- Salt – ½ tsp (2.5g)
- Pepper – ½ tsp (1.5g)
- Lemon juice – 1 tbsp. (15ml)
- Lemon zest –1 tsp (2g)

### Method:

1. Add lentils and half vegetable broth to a pan, bring it to boil and let it simmer until the lentil are tender and all water is absorbed
2. Boil bulgur into a separate pan with remaining broth, and let it simmer until the bulgur is done and all water is absorbed
3. Remove excess water, if left
4. Remove from heat, when bulgur is fluffy add it to the lentils
5. Add oil to a pan, light brown onions until fully tender and add pepper, mix well
6. Add the onion mixture to the lentil and bulgur
7. Add all other ingredients and stir
8. Garnish with parsley

**Nutrition per serving:** Calories - 119 | Fat 2.7g | Carbs 21.4g | Protein 4.5g | Sugar 2.6g | Potassium 215.9mg | Cholesterol – 0mg | Sodium – 525mg | Fiber – 13g

## 11.19 Creamy Lentils with Thyme & Spinach

Preparation Time - 5 minutes | Cooking Time - 60 minutes | Serves 3

### Ingredients:

- Olive oil – 2 tsp (10ml)
- Carrots (chopped) – 1 medium sized
- Garlic (crushed) – 2 cloves
- Onions (chopped) – 1 medium sized
- Bay leaf – 1
- Thyme – ½ bunch
- Lemon juice – 3 tbsp. (45g)
- Baby spinach – 1 cup (30g)
- Vegetable stock – 2 cup (473g)
- Coconut milk – 1 cup (237ml)

### Method:

1. Heat oil in a large pan, saute onions and carrots, then add garlic, half thyme and bay leaf
2. Add lentils, and stir thoroughly
3. Add vegetable stock, and let it simmer until lentils are tender and creamy
4. Stir in the spinach, thyme and milk, let it simmer until the spinach wilts
5. Stir in lemon juice, add more seasonings if desired
6. Serve hot!

**Nutrition per serving:** Calories - 71| Fat 4.55g| Carbs 7.65g| Protein 1.03g| Sugar 3.67g| Potassium 180.4mg | Cholesterol – 0mg |Sodium – 500mg |Fiber – 8g

## 11.20 Spicy Veggie Ramen with Tofu

Preparation Time - 15 minutes| Cooking Time - 50-60 minutes| Serves 4

### Ingredients:

- Mushrooms – 8 oz (227g)
- Egg-free ramen noodles – 1 ⅓ cup (133g)
- Soy sauce – 1 tbsp. (15g)
- Mirin – 1 tbsp. (15ml) (optional)
- Garlic clove – 1
- Spring onions (finely sliced) – 2
- Salt – to taste
- Ginger (grated) – 1 inch
- Bean sprouts – 2 cups (150g)
- Red chilies – finely sliced
- Kale – ½ cup (16g)
- Marinated tofu – 7 oz (198g)
- Garlic or chili oil – 2 tsp (10ml)

### Method:

1. Add ginger, garlic, chilies and mushrooms and saute
2. Add enough water, with soy, mirin and let boil until mushrooms are tender and fragrant
3. Strain excess water, and remove ginger and garlic, slice mushrooms
4. Blanch bean sprouts and kale
5. Boil the noodles in salted water, until tender, drain and pour in separate bowls
6. Heat mushrooms, marinated tofu, bean sprouts and kale to combine well
7. Divide the mixture evenly to the noodle bowls
8. Pour stock over, garnish with chilies and spring onions

**Nutrition per serving:**

Calories - 296.75| Fat 2.85g| Carbs 52.1g| Protein 15.95g| Sugar 3.75g| Potassium 445.5mg | Cholesterol – 0mg |Sodium – 835mg |Fiber – 4g

# 12 SIDES AND SMALL PLATES

## 12.1 Hungarian Paprika Potatoes

Preparation Time: 10 minutes| Cooking Time: 25 minutes| Serving: 4

**Ingredients:**

- Diced large potatoes – 4
- Minced garlic – 2 cloves
- Sour cream – ½ cup (115g)
- Olive oil – 2 tbsp (28ml)
- Chopped onion – 1
- Vegetable Broth – ¼ cup (60ml)
- Sweet paprika – 2 tbsp (14g)
- Cayenne pepper – ¼ tsp (0.5g)
- Fresh parsley – Garnishing
- Salt and pepper – To Taste

**Method:**

1. In a large skillet over medium-high heat, warm the olive oil. Add the chopped onion and garlic, cook for approximately 5 minutes.
2. Add the cayenne pepper, sweet paprika, and cubed potatoes to the skillet.
3. Add vegie broth and let it simmer for 20 to 25 minutes. Sour cream is added after the heat is turned off. To taste, add salt and pepper to the food.
4. Top with freshly chopped parsley while serving.

**Nutrition per serving:** Calories - 252| Fat - 11g | Carbs - 34g | Protein - 5g | Sugar – 4g | Potassium – mg | Cholesterol – 12mg | Sodium – 180mg | Fiber – 5g

## 12.2 Baked Brussel Sprouts

Preparation Time: 10 minutes| Cooking Time: 30 minutes| Serving: 4

**Ingredients:**

- Trimmed Brussel sprouts – 1 lb. (454g)
- Minced garlic – 2 cloves
- Vegetable broth – ½ cup (120ml)
- Honey – 1 tbsp (21g)
- Balsamic vinegar – 2 tbsp (30ml)
- Olive oil – 2 tbsp (28ml)
- Black pepper – ¼ tsp (0.6g)
- Salt – ½ tsp (3g)

**Method:**

1. Set the oven's temperature to 375°F (190°C).
2. After adding, sauté the garlic for one to two minutes until fragrant.
3. Stirring to mix, add the Brussels sprouts to the pan and season with salt and pepper.
4. The Brussels sprouts should be nicely browned after cooking them for 5-7 minutes while tossing periodically.
5. Blend the vegetable broth, balsamic vinegar, and honey in a small bowl. Over the Brussels sprouts, pour the mixture.

6. Once the liquid has thickened and the Brussels sprouts are cooked, place the pan in the oven for 20 to 25 minutes.
7. Serve warm.

**Nutrition per serving:** Calories - 130 | Fat - 7g | Carbs - 16g | Protein - 4g | Sugar - 9g | Potassium - mg | Cholesterol – 0mg | Sodium – 180mg | Fiber – 4g

## 12.3 Sesame Seed Asparagus

Preparation Time: 10 minutes | Cooking Time: 15 minutes | Serving: 4

**Ingredients:**
- Trimmed asparagus – 1 lb. (454g)
- Olive oil – 2tbsp (28ml)
- Sesame oil – 1 tbsp (14ml)
- Soy sauce – 1 tbsp (15ml)
- Sesame seeds – 1 tbsp (9g)
- Salt and pepper – To Taste

**Method:**
1. Set the oven's temperature to 400°F (200°C).
2. Combine the olive oil, sesame oil, soy sauce, sesame seeds, salt, and pepper in a small bowl.
3. After trimming the asparagus, spread it out on a baking sheet and cover it with the oil mixture. Toss well to coat everything equally.
4. The asparagus should be roasted in the preheated oven for 10 to 15 minutes, or until it is tender and the edges are just beginning to brown.
5. Serve warm.

**Nutrition per serving:**
Calories - 96 | Fat - 8g | Carbs - 5g | Protein – 3g | Sugar - g | Potassium - mg | Cholesterol – 0mg | Sodium – 248mg | Fiber – 3g

## 12.4 Sautéed Collard Ribbons

Preparation Time: 10 minutes | Cooking Time: 7 minutes | Serving: 4

**Ingredients:**
- Collard greens – 1 bunch
- Collard leaves – Thin slices
- Olive oil – 2 tbsp (28ml)
- Minced garlic – 2 cloves
- Red pepper flakes – ½ tsp (3g)
- Salt and pepper – To Taste
- Lemon juice – ½ lemon

**Method:**
1. A big skillet with medium heat is used to heat the olive oil.
2. Red pepper flakes and minced garlic should be added to the skillet and cooked for approximately a minute, or until aromatic.
3. Toss the collard greens with the garlic and oil in the pan after adding them.
4. Cook the collard greens for 5-7 minutes, stirring periodically, or until they are soft and wilted.

5. To taste, add salt and pepper to the food.

6. Toss the collard greens with the lemon juice to coat.

7. Serve hot.

**Nutrition per serving:** Calories - 88 | Fat - 7g | Carbs - 7g | Protein - 2g | Sugar – 1g | Potassium - mg | Cholesterol – 0mg |Sodium – 49mg | Fiber – 4g

## 12.5 Frijoles Refritos with Tomatoes

Preparation Time: 10 minutes | Cooking Time: 15 minutes | Serving: 4

**Ingredients:**

- Rinsed pinto beans – 1 can
- Diced tomato – 1 medium
- Diced onion – ½ small
- Minced garlic – 2 cloves
- Olive oil – 1 tbsp (28ml)
- Cumin powder – ½ tsp (2g)
- Chili powder – ½ tsp (2g)
- Salt and pepper – To Taste

**Method:**

1. Sauté the garlic and onions for two to three minutes, or until the onions are transparent.

2. Cook the diced tomato in the pan for a further two to three minutes while stirring periodically.

3. With a fork or potato masher, mash the pinto beans after adding them to the pot. Add seasonings.

4. The beans should be boiled through and somewhat thickened after an additional 5-7 minutes of cooking while stirring periodically.

5. Served hot, topped with cheese that has been grated, chopped cilantro, and, if preferred, a dollop of sour cream.

**Nutrition per serving:** Calories - 134 | Fat - 4g | Carbs - 20g | Protein - 6g | Sugar - 2g | Potassium - mg | Cholesterol – 0mg |Sodium – 267mg | Fiber – 6g

## 12.6 Sautéed Pesto Vegetables

Preparation Time: 10 minutes| Cooking Time: 15 minutes| Serving: 4

**Ingredients:**

- Olive oil – 2 tbsp (28g)
- Sliced onion – 1 small
- Minced garlic – 2 cloves
- Sliced red bell pepper – 1
- Sliced yellow bell pepper – 1
- Sliced zucchini – 1
- Sliced yellow squash – 1
- Pesto sauce – 2 tbsp (30g)
- Salt and pepper – to Taste

**Method:**

1. Sauté the garlic and onion together for two to three minutes, or until the onion is transparent.
2. When the veggies are soft, add the bell peppers, zucchini, and yellow squash to the skillet and continue to sauté for an additional 5-7 minutes while turning regularly.
3. Stir the pesto sauce into the pan after adding it.
4. To taste, add salt and pepper to the food.
5. Serve warm.

**Nutrition per serving:** Calories - 160| Fat - 11g | Carbs - 12g| Protein - 4g | Sugar - g | Potassium - mg | Cholesterol – mg |Sodium – 150mg | Fiber – 4g

## 12.7 Roasted Cauliflower

Preparation Time: 10 minutes| Cooking Time: 30 minutes| Serving: 4

**Ingredients:**

- Cauliflower head – 1
- Olive oil – 2 tbsp (28ml)
- Garlic powder – 1 tsp (3g)
- Paprika – 1 tsp (2.3g)
- Salt and pepper – To Taste
- Chopped parsley – 1 tbsp (4g)

**Method:**

1. Set the oven's temperature to 425°F (220°C).
2. Divided cauliflower into tiny florets and drizzle the olive oil and toss to coat.
3. Add the garlic powder, paprika, salt, and pepper.
4. Place the cauliflower on a baking sheet
5. Roast the cauliflower for 25 to 30 minutes, or until it is soft and golden brown, in the preheated oven.
6. Remove from the oven and top with fresh parsley.
7. Serve warm.

**Nutrition per serving:** Calories - 120| Fat - 10g | Carbs - 7g | Protein - 3g | Sugar - 3g | Potassium - mg | Cholesterol – 0mg |Sodium – 420mg |Fiber – 3g

## 12.8 Roasted Baby Turnips

Preparation Time: 10 minutes | Cooking Time: 30 minutes | Serving: 4

**Ingredients:**

- Trimmed baby turnips – 1 lb. (454g)
- Olive oil – 2 tbsp (28ml)
- Minced garlic – 2 cloves
- Dried thyme – 1 tbsp (3g)
- Salt and pepper – To Taste

**Method:**

1. Oven should be heated to 400°F (200°C).
2. Baby turnips should be well coated in olive oil, chopped garlic, and dry thyme before being placed in a big basin.
3. To taste, add salt and pepper to the food.
4. On a baking sheet, spread the turnips out in a single layer.
5. Turnips should be roasted for 25 to 30 minutes, regularly tossing, until they are soft and browned.

**Nutrition per serving:** Calories - 85 | Fat - 7g | Carbs - 6g | Protein - 1g | Sugar - 2g | Potassium - mg | Cholesterol – 0mg | Sodium – 100mg | Fiber – 2g

## 12.9 Tempeh Tacos

Preparation Time: 10 minutes | Cooking Time: 12 minutes | Serving: 2

**Ingredients:**

- Tempeh strips – 8
- Olive oil – 1 tbsp (28ml)
- Chili powder – 1 tsp (2.8g)
- Smoked paprika – 1 tsp (2.3g)
- Cumin – ½ tsp (1.4g)
- Garlic powder – ½ tsp (1.5g)
- Salt – ½ tsp (3g)
- Taco shells – 8
- Sliced avocado – 1
- Diced tomatoes – ½ cup (121g)
- Chopped cilantro – ¼ cup (4g)
- Diced red onion – ¼ cup (40g)
- Lime wedges – For Serving

**Method:**

1. Set the oven's temperature to 400°F (200°C). Cut the tempeh strips in half.
2. Mix all seasonings and brush it on the tempeh strips.
3. Until crispy and golden, bake for 10 to 12 minutes. Meanwhile, heat tacos.
4. Put two pieces of tempeh in each taco shell before putting the tacos together.
5. Add sliced avocado, diced tomatoes, cilantro and red onion on the top.
6. Lime wedges should be served alongside.

**Nutrition per serving:** Calories - 318| Fat - 19g | Carbs - 27g | Protein - 11g |Sugar - 2g| Potassium - mg | Cholesterol – mg |Sodium – 439mg |Fiber – 7g

## 12.10 Stuffed Sweet Potato

Preparation Time: 10 minutes| Cooking Time: 45 minutes| Serving: 4

### Ingredients:

- Sweet potatoes – 4 medium
- Rinsed black beans – 1 can
- Diced red bell pepper – 1
- Diced red onion – ½
- Frozen corn – ½ cup (82g)
- Shredded cheddar cheese – ½ cup (56g)
- Chopped fresh cilantro – ¼ cup (4g)
- Olive oil – 1 tbsp (14ml)
- Cumin – 1 tsp (2.6g)
- Chili powder – ½ tsp (1.4g)
- Salt and pepper – To Taste

### Method:

1. Turn on the oven to 400 °F (205 °C).
2. Bake them in the oven for 40–45 minutes after several fork pricks.
3. For 5-7 minutes, sauté chopped red onion and red bell pepper.
4. To the pan, add the black beans that have been rinsed and drained, cumin, chili powder, salt, and pepper. Cook the beans for a further 3–4 minutes, or until well heated.
5. The inside of the sweet potatoes may be softly mashed with a fork.
6. On top of the mashed sweet potatoes, spoon the bean and veggie combination. Return the filled sweet potatoes to the oven for an additional 5-7 minutes, or until the cheese has melted, and then sprinkle the cheese shreds on top.
7. Add corn and cilantro on top.

**Nutrition per serving:** Calories - 396| Fat - 10g | Carbs - 64g | Protein - 17g | Sugar - 16g | Potassium - mg | Cholesterol – 20mg |Sodium – 473mg |Fiber – 13g

## 12.11 Mashed Potatoes

Preparation Time: 10 minutes | Cooking Time: 15 minutes | Serving: 4

**Ingredients:**

- Chopped potatoes – 2 lb. (907g)
- Milk – ½ cup (120ml)
- Butter – 4 tbsp (58g)
- Salt and pepper – To Taste
- Parsley and chives – Garnishing

**Method:**

1. Bring enough water to cover the chopped potatoes to a boil in a big saucepan.
2. Once the water begins to boil, turn down the heat, cover, and simmer for approximately 15 minutes, or until the potatoes are fork-tender.
3. Potatoes are drained and added back to the saucepan.
4. Use a potato masher or a fork to mash the potatoes until they are smooth and creamy before adding the butter and milk to the saucepan.
5. Add salt and pepper to taste and serve with parsley and chives on top.

**Nutrition per serving:** Calories - 243 | Fat - 12g | Carbs - 31g | Protein - 4g | Sugar - g | Potassium - mg | Cholesterol – mg | Sodium – 158mg | Fiber – 3g

## 12.12 Sautéed Greens and Tamari

Preparation Time: 10 minutes | Cooking Time: 7 minutes | Serving: 2

**Ingredients:**

- Mix green – 2 cups (Collard, Chard, Spinach and Kale) (60g)
- Olive oil – 1 tbsp (14ml)
- Tamari – 1 tbsp (18g)
- Minced garlic – 1 clove
- Salt and pepper – To Taste

**Method:**

1. The mixed greens should be washed, dried, and chopped into bite-sized pieces.
2. Add the minced garlic to the pan and cook for about 30 seconds.
3. When the mixed greens are wilted but still somewhat crunchy, add them to the skillet and cook for a further 2 to 3 minutes.
4. Once the tamari has been absorbed and the greens are soft, drizzle more tamari over them and continue sautéing for an additional one to two minutes.
5. To taste, add salt and pepper to the food.

**Nutrition per serving:** Calories - 95 | Fat - 7g | Carbs - 6g | Protein - 3g | Sugar - 1g | Potassium - mg | Cholesterol – 0mg | Sodium – 545mg | Fiber – 3g

## 12.13 Hummus and Crudité Platter

Preparation Time: 10 minutes | Cooking Time: 10 minutes | Serving: 4

**Ingredients:**

- Hummus – 1 cup (240g)
- Sliced red bell pepper – 1
- Sliced yellow bell pepper – 1
- Sliced carrots – 2 medium
- Sliced cucumber – 1
- Sliced celery stalk – 1
- Sliced radish – 1 bunch
- Small grapes – 1 bunch

**Method:**

1. Put the prepared hummus on a dish or tray for serving.
2. Around the hummus, arrange the sliced bell peppers, carrots, cucumber, celery, radishes, and grapes in an appealing pattern.
3. Serve the plate without any dipping ingredients or with pita chips.

**Nutrition per serving:** Calories - 140 | Fat - 7g | Carbs - 16g | Protein - 5g | Sugar - 7g | Potassium - mg | Cholesterol – 0mg | Sodium – 260mg | Fiber – 5g

## 12.14 Glazed Radish

Preparation Time: 10 minutes | Cooking Time: 25 minutes | Serving: 4

**Ingredients:**

- Trimmed radish – 1 bunch
- Olive oil – 1 tbsp (14ml)
- Honey – 1 tbsp (21g)
- Soy sauce – 1 tbsp (18ml)
- Rice vinegar – 1 tbsp (15g)
- Minced garlic – 1 clove
- Salt and pepper – To Taste
- Sesame seeds – 1 tbsp (9g)
- Sliced green onion – 1

**Method:**

1. Set your oven's temperature to 375°F (190°C).
2. Olive oil, honey, soy sauce, rice vinegar, garlic, salt, and pepper should all be combined in a small bowl.
3. The radishes should be uniformly covered after being tossed in the glaze mixture.
4. Spread out the coated radishes in a single layer on a baking dish.
5. For 20 to 25 minutes, or until they are soft and caramelized, roast the radishes in the preheated oven.
6. Add chopped green onion and sesame seeds as a garnish.

**Nutrition per serving:** Calories - 63 | Fat - 3g | Carbs - 9g | Protein - 1g | Sugar - 7g | Potassium - mg | Cholesterol – mg | Sodium – 259mg | Fiber – 2g

# 13 SNACKS AND APPETIZERS

## 13.1 Halloumi & Pea Fritters

Preparation Time - 25 minutes | Cooking Time - 30 minutes | Serves 4

Ingredients:

- Halloumi – 8 oz (227g)
- Peas – 1 cup (240g)
- Greek yogurt – ¾ cup (170g)
- Eggs – 2
- Cumin seeds – 1 tsp (5g)
- Coconut milk – ¼ cup (60ml)
- Lemon – 2
- Dried chili flakes – 1 tsp (5g)
- Self-rising flour – ¼ cup (30g)
- Olive oil – 2 tbsp. (30ml)
- Chopped mint leaves – 1 tbsp. (1.6g)
- Salad leaves – to serve

Method:

1. Add peas to a bowl and crush them, add haloumi, milk, flour, mint, chili flakes and eggs, Mix together and season
2. Add 2 tbsp. of oil in a frying pan, once hot add around 4 tbsp. of fritter mixture heaped together to the pan
3. Flip over once one side is golden brown, and do the next side
4. Once done, place it in a platter, repeat the process with remaining mixture and make fritters
5. Serve hot with your favorite dip

**Nutrition per serving:** Calories - 400| Fat 26g| Carbs 20g| Protein 22g| Sugar 4g| Potassium 400mg| Cholesterol – 157mg |Sodium – 950mg | Fiber – 4g

## 13.2 Baked Cauliflower Florets

Preparation Time - 20 minutes | Cooking Time - 40 minutes | Serves 4

Ingredients:

- Cauliflower (cut into bite sized florets) – 1 medium sized
- Oregano – ½ tsp (2.5g)
- All-purpose flour – ½ cup (60g)
- Smoked paprika – 1 tsp (5g)
- Garlic (paste) – ½ tsp (2.5g)
- Almond milk – ⅓ cup (80ml)
- Vegetable oil – for spray
- Sweet chili sauce – 3 tbsp. (45g)
- Sriracha – 3 tbsp. (45g)
- Honey or maple syrup – 1 tbsp. (15g)
- Lemon juice – 3 tbsp. (45g)
- Spring onions (sliced) – 2
- Sesame seeds – 1 tbsp. (9g)

Method:

1. Heat the oven to 180°C (356°F), line a baking tray with baking paper.
2. Add breadcrumbs to a bowl
3. In a large bowl, add flour, oregano, garlic and seasoning along with paprika and whisk in milk to make batter with desired consistency
4. Add cauliflower florets to the batter, one-by-one to the batter and then breadcrumbs, coat them completely by tossing

5. Place the florets on the baking tray, and bake them together, with a spray of oil, until golden brown
6. Flip over the sides to avoid burning the upper side
7. In a pan combine, honey, sweet chili sauce, lemon juice and Sriracha, warm it by heating on medium heat
8. Toss the warm sauce mixture over the cauliflower florets into a platter
9. Garnish with sesame seeds and spring onions

**Nutrition per serving:** Calories - 240| Fat 8g| Carbs 38g| Protein 5g| Sugar 18g| Potassium 410mg| Cholesterol – 0mg |Sodium – 334mg | Fiber – 4g

## 13.3 Tofu Lemon Piccata

Preparation Time - 5 minutes| Cooking Time - 25 minutes| Serves 2

### Ingredients:

- Tofu block (extra-firm) – 9 oz (255g)
- Lemon juice – 2 tbsp. (30g)
- Olive oil – for frying
- Gram flour – 2 tbsp. (16g)
- Vegetable stock – ¼ cup (60ml)
- Capers – 1 tbsp. (15g)
- Peas – ½ cup (120g)
- Broccoli – ½ cup (60g)
- Parsley (small bunch) – ½ bunch

### Method:

1. Boil broccoli and peas for about 3 minutes in hot boiling water and drain
2. Place them in a shallow serving platter
3. Season the tofu and coat it in flour
4. Heat oil in a pan, and fry tofu and lemon together until light brown and crispy or as desired
5. Once done place them over the broccoli and peas
6. Meanwhile, Pour garlic to a pan and heat until fragrant, add wine and boil until a little less than half is left
7. Add stock and bring to boil until left by third, season according to taste
8. Remove from flame and whisk in olive oil, lemon and capers
9. Pour the sauce over the platter and serve

**Nutrition per serving:** Calories - 317| Fat 19g| Carbs 17g| Protein 22g| Sugar 4g| Potassium 501mg| Cholesterol – 0mg |Sodium – 289mg | Fiber – 6g

## 13.4 Vegetarian Tacos

Preparation Time - 10 minutes| Cooking Time - 30 minutes| Serves 4

### Ingredients:

- Smoked paprika – 2 tsp (10g)
- White vinegar – 5 tbsp. (75ml)
- Salad leaves – 8
- Red onion (sliced) – 1 medium sized
- Avocados – 1 medium sized
- Olive oil – 2 ½ tbsp. (37.5ml)
- Chipotle flakes – 1 tsp (5g)
- Cumin (ground) – 1 tsp (2g)
- Courgettes (sliced into 1 cm) – 2
- Black beans – 13 oz (369g)
- Garlic (chopped) – 2
- Coriander – 1 bunch
- Tortillas (of choice) – 8 small
- Lemon juice – 2 tbsp. (28ml)
- Yogurt – ½ cup (120g)

### Method:

1. Combine vinegar, onion and pinch of salt in a bowl and set aside
2. Add courgettes to a mixture of 1 tbsp. olive oil, cumin, flakes and paprika, and toss to coat completely
3. Put them in batches, into a frying pan with oil on medium-high heat and fry until deep brown
4. In the same frying pan add garlic, saute for a min then add beans and cook for few minutes with splashes of water if required, season to taste
5. Heat the tortillas
6. Mix yogurt, coriander, lemon juice and zest season to taste
7. Remove the onions from vinegar
8. Line up the tortillas, layer with salad leaves, sliced avocados, black beans and courgettes, drizzle over the lime yogurt
9. Serve with lemon wedges to squeeze

**Nutrition per serving:** Calories - 389| Fat 17g| Carbs 47g| Protein 16g| Sugar 3.75g| Potassium 1281mg| Cholesterol – 0mg |Sodium – 387mg | Fiber – 10.3g

## 13.5 Vegetarian Tempeh Kebabs

Preparation Time - 10 minutes | Cooking Time - 30 minutes | Serves 3

### Ingredients:

- Tempeh block – 10 oz (283g)
- Chili flakes – pinch
- Basil leaves – 1 tsp (5g)

### For Marination

- Umeboshi paste – 4 tbsp (60g)
- Soy sauce – 2 tbsp. (30ml)
- Garlic cloves (paste) – 2
- Sesame oil – 2 tsp (10ml)
- Shaoxing wine – 2 tsp (10ml)
- Chinese black vinegar – 2 tsp (10g)
- Dried chili flakes – ½ tsp (1g)
- Salt – to taste
- Chinese five spice powder – ½ tsp (2.5g)

### Method:

1. All all ingredients for marination to a food processor and blend until combined well
2. Cut tempeh into 3cm cubes
3. Pour over the marination material and marinate the tempeh, massaging all over and avoid breaking them
4. Put aside for 30 minutes
5. Skewer he tempeh, and grill it on a hot grill pan until nicely brown
6. Serve with garnishing with coriander and sprinkle of chili flakes

**Nutrition per serving:** Calories - 293 | Fat 14g | Carbs 17g | Protein 20g | Sugar 0.5g | Potassium 386mg | Cholesterol – 0mg | Sodium – 2103mg | Fiber – 7.9g

## 13.6 Balsamic-coated Brussels Sprouts

Preparation Time - 5 minutes | Cooking Time - 20 minutes | Serves 4

### Ingredients:

- Brussels sprouts (halved) – 2 ½ cups (400g)
- Balsamic vinegar – 1 cup (240ml)
- Onion (diced) – 1 large
- Olive oil – 1 tsp (5ml)
- Brown rice syrup – ¼ cup (60g)
- Sea salt – to taste
- Black pepper – to taste

### Method:

1. Place balsamic vinegar on medium-high heat and heat until left ½ cup
2. Steam brussels sprouts, until tender
3. Meanwhile, saute onions in olive oil until light brown
4. Add prepared vinegar, syrup and brussels sprouts, season with salt and pepper, mix well
5. Heat for 5 minutes, serve hot!

**Nutrition per serving:** Calories - 126 | Fat 2.3g | Carbs 24g | Protein 3g | Sugar 13g | Potassium 529mg | Cholesterol – 0mg | Sodium – 78mg | Fiber – 4g

## 13.7 Garlic Mushroom & Greens

Preparation Time - 5 minutes | Cooking Time - 30 minutes | Serves 3

### Ingredients:

- Mushrooms – 7 oz (198g)
- Green beans – 1 cup (110g)
- Garlic – 6 cloves
- Sesame seeds – 1 tsp (2.5g)
- Vegetable broth – 2 tbsp. (30g)
- Tamari salt – to taste

### Method:

1. Trim the ends of beans and cut them into 1 inch pieces
2. Steam over boiling water until tender
3. Heat vegetable broth on medium high heat, add sesame seeds and saute garlic
4. Add mushrooms and beans, season with salt
5. Cook for few minutes until creamy
6. Serve and enjoy!

**Nutrition per serving:** Calories - 51 | Fat 1.8g | Carbs 6.5g | Protein 3.3g | Sugar 1.9g | Potassium 331mg | Cholesterol – 0mg | Sodium – 210mg | Fiber – 2.7g

## 13.8 Roasted Asparagus

Preparation Time - 7 minutes | Cooking Time - 12 minutes | Serves 3

### Ingredients:

- Asparagus (ends removed) – 8 oz (227g)
- Sea salt – ½ tsp (2.5g)
- Fennel seeds – ½ tsp (1g)
- Black pepper – ½ tsp (1.5g)
- Fresh oregano (chopped) – 2 tbsp. (6g)
- Lemon juice – 2 tbsp (30ml)
- Lemon wedges – of 1 lemon
- Olive oil – 1 tbsp. (15ml)

### Method:

1. Heat oven at 450°F (230 °C)
2. Combine all ingredients in a bowl, marinate asparagus
3. Coat the asparagus
4. Bake for 10-12 minutes or until crispy
5. Garnish with lemon wedges

**Nutrition per serving:** Calories - 296.75 | Fat 2.85g | Carbs 52.1g | Protein 15.95g | Sugar 3.75g | Potassium 445.5mg | Cholesterol – 32mg | Sodium – 195mg | Fiber – 2.6g

# 13.9 Onion Rings

Preparation Time - 2 minutes | Cooking Time - 12 minutes | Serves 1

## Ingredients:

- Onion (sliced round to have rings) – 1 large
- Eggs – 2
- Basil leaves (dried) – 1 tsp (0.5g)
- Bread crumbs – ½ cup (28g)

## For Marination

- Corn flour – 3 tbsp. (28.5g)
- Salt – to taste
- Chili flakes – ½ tsp (1g)
- Red pepper – to taste
- Cumin seeds – 1 tsp (2g)
- Lemon juice – 1 tbsp. (15ml)
- Soy sauce – 1 tbsp. (15ml)

## Method:

1. Mix all marination ingredients and form thick paste, use water if required
2. Whisk eggs in a bowl, and place bread crumbs in a separate bowl
3. Dip onion rings in the mixture, dip in eggs and then coat with crumbs
4. Shallow fry or air-fry until golden brown
5. Serve by sprinkle of basil leaves on top, with any dip

**Nutrition per serving:** Calories - 60 | Fat 4.5g | Carbs 5g | Protein 2g | Sugar 2g | Potassium 280mg | Cholesterol – 372mg | Sodium – 1449mg | Fiber – 6.9g

# 13.10 Tofu nuggets

Preparation Time - 10 minutes | Cooking Time - 15 minutes | Serves 4

## Ingredients:

- Tofu (extra-firm) – 14 oz (397g)
- Onion powder – 1 tsp (2.1g)
- Garlic powder – 1 tbsp. (8.3g)
- Paprika – 1 tsp (2.5g)
- Veggie broth powder – 1 tsp (5g)
- Water – ⅓ cup (80ml)
- Soy sauce – 2 tbsp. (30g)
- Nutritional yeast – ⅓ cup (30g)

## Method:

1. Preheat the airfryer at 400°F (200°C)
2. Press tofu for 10-30 minutes
3. Add all ingredients to a bowl and make a paste (add water if it is thick and yeast if it is too thin)
4. Cut tofu into bite-sized pieces and bend them a little with hands to let the paste stay over
5. Dip the tofu in paste and place them in air fryer basket
6. Fry for 10-15 minutes or more for desired results
7. Serve hot with any sauce of choice

**Nutrition per serving:** Calories - 166 | Fat 6.5g | Carbs 11.5g | Protein 18.5g | Sugar 1.5g | Potassium 336mg | Cholesterol – 0mg | Sodium – 689mg | Fiber – 1.5g

## 13.11 Pinwheel tortilla bites

Preparation Time - 2 minutes | Cooking Time - 12 minutes | Serves 1

### Ingredients:

- Grain tortillas – 2
- Lettuce leaves – 2
- Shredded carrots – 1 medium sized
- Hummus – ½ cup (130g)
- Shredded bell pepper (of choice) – 2 tbsp. (20g)

### Method:

1. Place tortilla on a plain surface, spread dip all over it evenly
2. Spread veggies with lettuce leaves being the first and carrots, bell pepper and broccoli slaw
3. Roll up the tortilla to the edge, and cut it out into bit sized pinwheels
4. Serve with any dip or hummus

### Nutrition per serving:

Calories - 361 | Fat 14g | Carbs 50g | Protein 12g | Sugar 7g | Potassium 508mg | Cholesterol – 0mg | Sodium – 935mg | Fiber – 12g

## 13.12 Kale bites

Preparation Time - 2 minutes | Cooking Time - 12 minutes | Serves 1

### Ingredients:

- Baguette (egg -free) (with small width to have bite sized pieces)
- Kale – 2 cup (130g)
- Garlic powder – 2 tsp (5g)
- Olive oil – 2 tsp (10g)
- Balsamic vinegar – 1 tbsp. (15g)
- Pepper – to taste
- Mayonnaise – as required
- Shredded carrots – 1 medium sized
- Shredded bell pepper – 1 medium sized
- Avocado – 2 medium sized

### Method:

1. Cut baguette into slices
2. Heat olive oil and saute kale with garlic powder, add vinegar and pepper, let it cook until kale wilts
3. Press it down to form paste
4. Spread mayonnaise layer and kale paste on baguette slices, place avocado slices on one side and carrot and bell pepper shreds on other side
5. Serve with any sauce of choice

### Nutrition per serving:

Calories - 448 | Fat 28.5g | Carbs 44g | Protein 9g | Sugar 6.5g | Potassium 742mg | Cholesterol – 0mg | Sodium – 270mg | Fiber – 7g

## 13.13 Ricotta Basil Balls

Preparation Time – 15 minutes | Cooking Time - 15 minutes | Serves – 2

### Ingredients

- All-purpose flour – 2 tbsp.
- Chives – 1 tbsp (2.5g)
- Basil – ½ oz. (14g)
- Commercial egg replacer – 1½ tsp (6ml)
- Ricotta – 9 oz. (255g) (crumbled)
- Breadcrumbs – For Coating
- Salt and pepper – To Taste

### Method

1. Combine commercial egg replacer, basil, chives, flour and ricotta in a bowl.
2. Knead all ingredients to make a mixture and form 20 balls.
3. Pour balls in flour mixture and then coat with breadcrumbs.
4. Air fry all the balls in 2 different batches for 8 minutes at 390°F (199°C) and serve warm.

**Nutrition per serving:** Calories - 69 | Fat 3g | Carbs 7g | Protein 4.4g | Sugar 0.5g | Potassium 55mg | Cholesterol – 24mg | Sodium – 78mg | Fiber – 0.3g

## 13.14 Mushroom Mini Wedges

Preparation Time – 10 minutes | Cooking Time - 24 minutes | Serves – 8

### Ingredients

- Mushroom – 4 ½ oz (127g)
- Ground pepper – To Taste
- Pie crust – 3 ½ oz. (99g)
- Oil – ½ tbsp. (7.5ml)
- Vegan cheese – 1.4 oz. (40g)
- Vegan whipped cream – 3 tbsp. (45g)

### Method

1. Cut pie crust with a cookie cutter and place crust in a mold.
2. Pour mushrooms, cheese and cream over the pie crust.
3. Preheat air fryer at 390°F (199°C) and then cook the pie crust for 12 minutes.
4. Take out the pie crust and cut each pie into half and serve tem hot.
5. Enjoy!

**Nutrition per serving:** Calories - 112 | Fat 8.5g | Carbs 6.3g | Protein 3g | Sugar 0.8g | Potassium 81mg | Cholesterol – 32mg | Sodium – 113mg | Fiber – 0.3g

## 13.15 Vegan Parmesan Potato Croquettes

Preparation Time – 20 minutes | Cooking Time - 30 minutes | Serves – 4

**Ingredients**

- Diced large potatoes – 3
- Vegan parmesan cheese – ½ cup (40g)
- Chopped fresh parsley – ¼ cup (15g)
- Chopped onion – ¼ cup (40g)
- Minced garlic – 2 cloves
- All-purpose flour – ½ cup (60g)
- Breadcrumbs – ½ cup (60g)
- Salt – 1 tsp (5g)
- Black pepper – ½ tsp (1.55g)
- Vegetable oil – ¼ cup (60ml)

**Method**

1. Boil the diced potatoes in a big saucepan for 15 to 20 minutes, or until they are soft. After draining the water, place the potatoes in a big basin.
2. To the bowl of boiling potatoes, add the vegan Parmesan cheese, vegan mayonnaise, parsley, onion, and garlic. All of the ingredients should be well mixed.
3. Combine the breadcrumbs, all-purpose flour, salt, and black pepper in a separate bowl.
4. The potato mixture should be formed into little croquettes.
5. Each croquette should be well covered in the flour and breadcrumb mixture.
6. In a big frying pan, heat the vegetable oil on medium-high. The croquettes should be added to the pan after the oil is heated and fried for two to three minutes each side, or until they are golden brown on both sides.
7. The croquettes should be taken out of the pan using a slotted spoon and placed on a dish covered with paper towels to soak up any extra oil.
8. The croquettes should be served hot with your preferred dipping sauce.

**Nutrition per serving:** Calories - 345 | Fat 16g | Carbs 42g | Protein 7g | Sugar 2g | Potassium mg | Cholesterol – 0mg | Sodium – 784mg | Fiber – 5g

## 13.16 Mushroom Mini Wedges

Preparation Time – 10 minutes| Cooking Time - 24 minutes| Serves – 8

**Ingredients**

- Potatoes (boiled) – 4
- Sweet corn – ½ cup (90g)
- Green peas – ½ cup (80g)
- Bell pepper – ½ cup (75g)
- Cauliflower rice – ½ cup (50g)
- Onion (finely chopped) – ¼ cup (40g)
- Coriander leaves – 2 tsp (2g)
- Chili flakes – 2 tsp (3g)
- Oregano – 2 tsp (2g)
- Bread crumbs – ½ cup (60g)
- Salt – to taste
- Coriander powder – ½ tsp (2g)
- Chat masala – ½ tsp (2g)
- Ginger garlic paste – 1 tsp (5g)
- For Coating
- Refined flour – 2 tbsp (16g)
- Corn starch – 2 tbsp (16g)
- Bread crumbs – ½ cup (60g)
- Red chili powder – ¼ tsp (0.5g)

**Method**

1. Add the mashed potatoes, finely chopped vegetables, ginger garlic paste, and spices to a mixing bowl.
2. Add the bread crumbs and combine well.
3. Take out a few tiny roundels or balls after greasing your hands.
4. Now combine refined flour and corn starch to create a slurry.
5. Add a dash of salt and red chilli powder.
6. Roll the vegetable balls in bread crumbs after dipping them in the slurry.
7. Once more, dunk it in the slurry, and then coat it with bread crumbs.
8. Repeat with all the balls.
9. In a deep frying pan, heat the oil.
10. Fry the coated vegetable balls till crisp and golden.
11. To remove extra oil, remove from the oil and place on a paper serviette.
12. Serve with your choice of hot sauce or dip.

**Nutrition per serving:** Calories - 201| Fat 1.8g| Carbs 41.8g| Protein 6.2g| Sugar 4.9g| Potassium 641.5mg |Cholesterol – 0mg |Sodium – 259.5mg | Fiber – 5.2g

# 14 SMOOTHIES RECIPES

## 14.1 Blueberry Banana Smoothie

Preparation Time: 5 minutes | Cooking Time: 0 minutes | Serving: 1

**Ingredients:**

- Banana – 1
- Blueberry – 1 cup (148g)
- Spinach – ½ cup (15g)
- Water – ½ cup (120ml)
- Chia seeds – 1 tbsp. (12g)
- Almond milk – ½ cup (120ml)

**Method:**

1. Pour all ingredients into a blender.
2. Blend them until they are smooth.
3. Pour smoothie in a glass and enjoy.

**Nutrition per serving:**

Calories - 220 | Fat - 7g | Carbs - 39g | Protein - 4g | Sugar - 20g | Potassium - 1074mg | Cholesterol – 0mg | Sodium – 95mg | Fiber – 8g

## 14.2 Peach Raspberry Smoothie

Preparation Time: 5 minutes | Cooking Time: 0 minutes | Serving: 1

**Ingredients:**

- Raspberries – 1 cup (148g)
- Spinach – ½ cup (15g)
- Peach – 1 (sliced)
- Almond milk – ½ cup (120ml)
- Flaxseeds – 1 tbsp. (12g)
- Water – ½ cup (120ml)

**Method:**

1. Pour everything in a blender and blend.
2. Smoothie is ready to serve.

**Nutrition per serving:**

Calories - 200 | Fat - 6g | Carbs - 36g | Protein - 4g | Sugar - 21g | Potassium - 871mg | Cholesterol – 0mg | Sodium – 52mg | Fiber – 10g

## 14.3 Detoxifying Green Machine

Preparation Time: 5 minutes | Cooking Time: 0 minutes | Serving: 1

**Ingredients:**

- Banana – 1
- Grapes – ½ cup (75g)
- Parsley – ½ cup (30g)
- Kale – ½ cup (30g)
- Water – 6 ounces (177ml)
- Flaxseeds – 1 tsp. (2.5g)

**Method:**

1. Add all ingredient in a blender and blend them smoothly.
2. Ready to serve.

**Nutrition per serving:**

Calories - 180 | Fat - 3g | Carbs - 38g | Protein - 8g | Sugar - 17g | Potassium - 948mg | Cholesterol – 0mg | Sodium – 78mg | Fiber – 7g

## 14.4 Pear and Spiced Blueberry Smoothie

Preparation Time: 5 minutes | Cooking Time: 0 minutes | Serving: 1

**Ingredients:**

- Pear – 1
- Cinnamon grounded – ¼ tsp. (0.6g)
- Frozen blueberries – 1 cup (148g)
- Almond milk – 4 ounces (118ml)
- Ground nutmeg – ¼ tsp (0.6g)

**Method:**

1. Pour everything in a blender and blend.
2. Smoothie is ready to serve.

**Nutrition per serving:**

Calories - 208 | Fat - 1g | Carbs - 49g | Protein - 2g | Sugar - 26g | Potassium - 466mg | Cholesterol – 0mg | Sodium – 74mg | Fiber – 9g

## 14.5 Peach Mango Smoothie

Preparation Time: 5 minutes| Cooking Time: 0 minutes| Serving: 1

**Ingredients:**

- Peach – 1
- Mango – ½
- Rainbow chard leaves – 3 (large)
- Vanilla extract – ¼ tsp. (0.6g)
- Almond milk – 4 ounces (118ml)

**Method:**

1. Add all ingredient in a blender and blend them smoothly.
2. Ready to serve.

**Nutrition per serving:** Calories - 293| Fat - 1g | Carbs - 37g | Protein -9g | Sugar - 29g | Potassium - 702mg | Cholesterol – 0mg |Sodium – 81mg |Fiber – 9g

## 14.6 Mango Pineapple Smoothie

Preparation Time: 5 minutes| Cooking Time: 0 minutes| Serving: 1

**Ingredients:**

- Frozen pineapple – 1
- Frozen mango – 1
- Coconut milk – ½ cup (120ml)
- Spinach – ½ cup (15g)
- Hemp seeds – 1 tbsp. (12g)
- Water – ½ cup (120ml)

**Method:**

1. Pour everything in a blender and blend.
2. Smoothie is ready to serve.

**Nutrition per serving:** Calories - 260| Fat - 12g | Carbs - 34g | Protein - 6g | Sugar - 23g | Potassium - 624mg | Cholesterol – 0mg |Sodium – 34mg |Fiber – 6g

## 14.7 Peanut Butter Chocolate Smoothie

Preparation Time: 5 minutes| Cooking Time: 0 minutes| Serving: 1

**Ingredients:**

- Cocoa powder – 1 tbsp. (12g)
- Peanut butter – 2 tbsp. (32g)
- Banana – 1
- Water – ½ cup (120ml)
- Almond milk – ½ cup (120ml)
- Flaxseeds – 1 tbsp. (12g)

**Method:**

1. Add all ingredient in a blender and blend them smoothly.
2. Ready to serve.

**Nutrition per serving:** Calories - 484| Fat - 21g | Carbs - 50g | Protein - 16g | Sugar - 23g | Potassium - 679mg | Cholesterol – 0mg |Sodium – 102mg | Fiber – 11g

## 14.8 Green Smoothie

Preparation Time: 5 minutes| Cooking Time: 0 minutes| Serving: 1

**Ingredients:**

- Banana – 1
- Avocado – ½
- Spinach – 1 cup (30g)
- Almond milk – ½ cup (120ml)
- Chia seeds – 1 tbsp. (12g)

**Method:**

1. Pour everything in a blender and blend.
2. Smoothie is ready to serve.

**Nutrition per serving:** Calories - 355| Fat - 21g | Carbs - 36g | Protein - 7g | Sugar - 13g | Potassium - 943mg | Cholesterol – 0mg |Sodium – 131mg |Fiber – 14g

## 14.9 Berry Blast

Preparation Time: 5 minutes| Cooking Time: 0 minutes| Serving: 1

**Ingredients:**

- Banana – 1
- Rolled oats – ¼ cup (20g)
- Frozen mixed berries – 1 cup (148g)
- Almond milk – ½ cup (120ml)
- Honey – 1 tbsp. (15ml)

**Method:**

1. Pour everything in to blender and blend.
2. Smoothie is ready to serve.

**Nutrition per serving:** Calories - 307| Fat - 3g | Carbs - 64g | Protein - 6g | Sugar - 29g | Potassium - 603mg | Cholesterol – 0mg | Sodium – 86mg |Fiber – 10g

## 14.10 Ginger Fruity Smoothie

Preparation Time: 10 minutes| Cooking Time: 5 minutes| Serving: 1

**Ingredients:**

- Baby spinach – 1 cup (30g)
- Ginger – 1 tsp. (12g)
- Sliced Peaches – 2 cups (340g)
- Honey – 2 tbsp. (30ml)
- Water – 1 ¼ cup (296ml)

**Method:**

1. Air fry peaches for 5 minutes at 370° F.
2. Let it cool.
3. Pour everything in a blender and blend, smoothie is ready to serve.

**Nutrition per serving:** Calories - 87| Fat – 0.5g | Carbs - 21g | Protein – 1.9g | Sugar – 19.8g | Potassium - 386mg | Cholesterol – 0mg |Fiber – 2.8g | Sodium – 17mg

## 14.11 Turmeric Pineapple Smoothie

Preparation Time: 5 minutes | Cooking Time: 0 minutes | Serving: 1

### Ingredients:

- Banana – 1
- Turmeric – ½ tsp. (1.5ml)
- Ground ginger – ½ tsp. (1.5ml)
- Vanilla extract – ½ tsp. (2.5ml)
- Frozen pineapple – 1 cup (165g)
- Unsweet almond milk – 1 cup (237ml)

### Method:

1. Blend together almond milk, frozen pineapple, banana, turmeric, ginger, and vanilla essence.
2. Once smooth, blend.
3. Pour into a glass, then sip.

### Nutrition per serving:

Calories - 195 | Fat - 3g | Carbs - 43g | Protein - 3g | Sugar -24g | Potassium - mg | Cholesterol – 0mg | Sodium – 19mg | Fiber – 6g

## 14.12 Cherry Chocolate Smoothie

Preparation Time: 5 minutes | Cooking Time: 0 minutes | Serving: 1

### Ingredients:

- Banana – 1
- Frozen cherries – 1 cup (148g)
- Almond butter – 1 tbsp. (16g)
- Unsweet cocoa powder – 1 tbsp. (12g)
- Unsweet vanilla almond milk – 1 cup (237ml)

### Method:

1. Blend together the frozen cherries, banana, cocoa powder, almond milk, and almond butter.
2. Once smooth, blend.
3. Pour into a glass, then sip.

### Nutrition per serving:

Calories - 267 | Fat - 12g | Carbs - 41g | Protein - 7g | Sugar - 22g | Potassium - mg | Cholesterol – 0mg | Sodium – 13mg | Fiber – 9g

# 15 DESSERTS

## 15.1 Apple Berry Crumble

Preparation Time: 20 minutes | Cooking Time: 40 minutes | Serving: 6

### Ingredients:

### For Filling

- Chopped apples – 3 medium
- Mixed berries – 1 cup (150g)
- All-purpose flour – 2 tbsp. (15g)
- Granulated sugar – ¼ cup (50g)
- Ground cinnamon – ½ tsp (4g)
- Ground nutmeg – ¼ tsp (2g)

### For Crumble Topping

- All-purpose flour – 1 cup (120g)
- Rolled oats – ½ cup (40g)
- Brown sugar – ½ cup (110g)
- Unsalted butter – ½ cup (113g)
- Ground cinnamon – ½ tsp (4g)
- Salt – ¼ tsp (2g)

### Method:

1. Set your oven's temperature to 375°F (190°C).
2. The diced apples, mixed berries, flour, sugar, cinnamon, and nutmeg should all be thoroughly blended in a medium-sized basin.
3. Fill an 8x8-inch baking dish with the fruit mixture, and then place it aside.
4. The flour, rolled oats, brown sugar, butter, cinnamon, and salt should all be combined in a separate basin. Blend well until crumbly.
5. Over the fruit mixture, evenly distribute the crumble mixture.
6. Bake for 35 to 40 minutes, or until the fruit filling is bubbling and the crumble topping is golden brown.
7. Before serving, take it out of the oven and allow it to cool for a while.

### Nutrition per serving:

Calories - 360 | Fat - 16g | Carbs - 53g | Protein - 3g | Sugar - 31g | Potassium – 157mg | Cholesterol – 40mg | Sodium – 105mg | Fiber – 4g

## 15.2 Pumpkin Pie

Preparation Time: 10 minutes | Cooking Time: 55 minutes | Serving: 8

### Ingredients:

- 9-inch pie crust – 1
- Pumpkin puree – 1 can (15 ounces)
- Commercial Egg Replacer – 2 tbsp. (30ml)
- Water – 6 tbsp. (90ml)
- Ground cinnamon – 1 tsp (8g)
- Ground ginger – ½ tsp
- Ground nutmeg – ½ tsp (4g)
- Salt – ½ tsp (2g)
- Whipped cream - Serving

### Method:

1. Turn on the oven to 425 °F (218 °C).
2. Pumpkin puree, sweetened condensed milk, egg replacer, water, cinnamon, ginger, nutmeg, and salt should all be thoroughly combined in a large mixing basin.
3. Stir the ingredients evenly after pouring it into the pie shell.
4. A toothpick put into the center of the pie should come out clean after 35 to 40 minutes of baking at 350°F (177°C) after 15 minutes of initial baking.
5. Before serving, take the pie out of the oven and allow it to cool to room temperature.
6. If you like, serve with whipped cream.

**Nutrition per serving:** Calories - 313 | Fat - 14g | Carbs - 41g | Protein - 8g | Sugar - 30g | Potassium - 64mg | Cholesterol – 65mg | Sodium – 331mg | Fiber – 2g

## 15.3 Ginger Bread

Preparation Time: 15 minutes | Cooking Time: 35 minutes | Serving: 12

### Ingredients:

- All-purpose flour – 2 cups (240g)
- Baking soda – 1 tsp (8g)
- Ground ginger – 1 tsp (8g)
- Ground cinnamon – 1 tsp (8g)
- Ground nutmeg – ¼ tsp (2g)
- Salt – ¼ tsp (2g)
- Salted butter – ½ cup (115g)
- Brown sugar – ½ cup (110)
- Molasses – ½ cup
- Commercial egg replacer – 1 tbsp. (15ml)
- Water – 3 tbsp. (45ml)
- Hot water – ½ cup (118ml)

### Method:

1. Set the oven's temperature to 350°F (180°C). A 9-inch square baking pan should be greased.
2. Mix the ingredients evenly.
3. To the butter mixture, add the molasses and egg, and beat until thoroughly incorporated.

4. Mix thoroughly after gradually including the dry components into the butter and add hot water.

5. Bake for 30-35 minutes and serve.

**Nutrition per serving:** Calories - 202| Fat - 7g | Carbs - 33g | Protein - 2g | Sugar - 18g | Potassium - 174mg | Cholesterol – 33mg |Sodium – 183mg | Fiber – 1g

## 15.4 Chocolate Avocado Pudding

Preparation Time: 10 minutes| Cooking Time: 0 minutes| Serving: 4

**Ingredients:**

- Ripe avocados – 2
- Cocoa powder – ¼ cup (21g)
- Maple syrup – ¼ cup (59ml)
- Almond milk – ¼ cup (59ml)
- Vanilla extract – 1 tsp (5ml)

**Method:**

1. Remove the pit from the avocados, cut them in half, and scoop the flesh into a blender.

2. Blend cocoa powder, maple syrup, almond milk, and vanilla essence.

3. Blend the ingredients up until they're creamy and smooth.

4. Cool it before serving.

**Nutrition per serving:**

Calories - 194| Fat - 13g | Carbs - 23g | Protein - 3g | Sugar - 12g | Potassium - 717mg | Cholesterol – 0mg |Sodium – 11mg | Fiber – 7g

## 15.5 Peanut Butter Cookies

Preparation Time: 10 minutes| Cooking Time: 12 minutes| Serving: 12

**Ingredients:**

- Creamy peanut butter – 1 cup (240g)
- Brown sugar – ½ cup (110g)
- Ground flaxseed – 1 tbsp. (8g)
- Water – 3 tbsp. (45ml)
- Vanilla extract – 1 tsp (5ml)

**Method:**

1. A baking sheet should be lined with parchment paper and the oven should be preheated to 350°F (180°C).

2. The peanut butter, brown sugar, flax egg, and vanilla extract should all be combined in a mixing dish.

3. Scoop tablespoon-sized balls of dough from the bowl and arrange them on the baking sheet.

4. For 10 to 12 minutes, or until golden brown, bake the cookies.

5. Cool the cookies and serve them.

**Nutrition per serving:**

Calories - 178| Fat - 12g | Carbs - 14g | Protein - 6g | Sugar - 10g | Potassium - 161mg | Cholesterol – 0mg | Sodium – 14mg | Fiber – 2g

## 15.6 Blueberry Oatmeal Bar

Preparation Time: 10 minutes| Cooking Time: 35 minutes| Serving: 9

**Ingredients:**

- Rolled oats – 2 cups (160g)
- Almond flour – 1 cup (96g)
- Maple syrup – ½ cup (118ml)
- Melted coconut oil – ¼ cup (59ml)
- Vanilla extract – 1 tsp (5ml)
- Frozen blueberries – 1 cup (140g)

**Method:**

1. To begin, line an 8-inch square baking dish with parchment paper and preheat the oven to 350°F (180°C).
2. Combined all ingredients in a mixing dish.
3. Stir carefully after adding the blueberries to the basin.
4. With a spatula, transfer the mixture to the baking dish and level it out.
5. For 30-35 minutes, or until golden brown, bake the bars.
6. Serve the bars by cutting them into squares.

**Nutrition per serving:** Calories - 293| Fat - 16g | Carbs - 32g | Protein - 7g | Sugar - 14g | Potassium - 102mg | Cholesterol – 0mg | Sodium – 0.6mg | Fiber – 5g

## 15.7 Banana Nut Muffins

Preparation Time: 15 minutes| Cooking Time: 25 minutes| Serving: 12

**Ingredients:**

- Ripe bananas – 2 (mashed)
- Coconut oil – ¼ cup (59ml)
- Maple syrup – ¼ cup (59ml)
- Almond milk – ¼ cup (59ml)
- Vanilla extract – 1 tsp (5ml)
- Whole wheat flour – 6.35 ounces (180g)
- Chopped walnuts – ½ cup (50g)
- Baking powder – 1 tsp (8g)
- Baking soda – ½ tsp (4g)
- Salt – ½ (4g)

**Method:**

1. Set the oven's temperature to 350°F (175°C).
2. The mashed bananas, melted coconut oil, maple syrup, almond milk, and vanilla extract should all be combined in a large mixing dish.
3. Combine the flour, walnuts, baking powder, baking soda and salt in a separate basin.
4. Use muffin liners or coconut oil to grease a muffin pan. Add batter to each muffin cup until it is 3/4 filled.
5. A toothpick put into the center of a muffin should come out clean after 20 to 25 minutes of baking.
6. Serve warm.

**Nutrition per serving:** Calories - 198| Fat - g | Carbs - 25g | Protein - g | Sugar – 8g|Potassium - 82mg| Cholesterol – 0mg | Sodium – 1955mg | Fiber – 3g

## 15.8 No-Cook Vegan Tiramisu

Preparation Time: 20 minutes| Chilling Time: 2 hours| Serving: 6

**Ingredients:**

- Soaked overnight cashews – 1 cup (150g)
- Almond milk – ½ cup (118ml)
- Maple syrup – ¼ cup (59ml)
- Coconut oil – 2 tbsp. (30ml)
- Vanilla extract – 1 tsp (5ml)
- Salt – ½ tsp (4g)
- Vegan ladyfingers – 24
- Brewed coffee – ½ cup (118ml)
- Cocoa powder – ¼ cup (21g)

**Method:**

1. Grind all ingredients in the processor.
2. One at a time, dip the ladyfingers into the cooled coffee, being care to fully cover them.
3. Put the soaked ladyfingers in a single layer in a 9 × 9inch baking dish.
4. Spread out the remaining half of the cashew cream mixture equally over the ladyfingers.
5. Continue adding layers.
6. The dish should be wrapped in plastic wrap and chilled in the fridge for at least two hours or overnight.
7. Dust the tiramisu with chocolate powder before serving.

**Nutrition per serving:**
Calories - 336| Fat - 20g | Carbs - 33g | Protein - 6g | Sugar - 16g | Potassium - 277mg | Cholesterol –0 mg | Sodium – 258mg | Fiber – 2g

## 15.9 Raspberry Coconut Panna Cotta

Preparation Time: 10 minutes | Cooking Time: 10 minutes | Chilling Time: 4 hours | Serving: 4

### Ingredients:

- Full-fat coconut milk – 1 can (400ml)
- Frozen raspberries – ½ cup (70g)
- Maple syrup – ¼ cup (59ml)
- Vanilla extract – 1 tsp (5ml)
- Agar agar powder – 1 tbsp. (8g)
- Shredded coconut – ¼ cup (20g)

### Method:

1. The raspberries should be pureed in a blender until smooth.
2. The coconut milk, maple syrup, and vanilla extract should be simmering in a saucepan over medium heat.
3. Stir thoroughly after adding the agar agar powder to the pan.
4. Stirring occasionally, lower the heat to a simmer for 5 to 7 minutes, or until the agar agar powder has completely dissolved.
5. Blend thoroughly after adding the raspberry puree to the pan.
6. Four glasses or ramekins should receive the mixture.
7. Set the product in the refrigerator for at least 4 hours.
8. Serve with coconut shavings on top.

**Nutrition per serving:** Calories - 287 | Fat - 23g | Carbs - 21g | Protein - 2g | Sugar - 13g | Potassium - 465mg | Cholesterol – 0mg | Sodium – 26mg | Fiber – 3g

## 15.10 Grape Focaccia

Preparation Time: 15 minutes | Cooking Time: 25 minutes | Serving: 8

### Ingredients:

- All-purpose flour – 2 cups (240g)
- Active dry yeast – 1 tsp (7g)
- Salt – 1 tsp (8g)
- Sugar – 1 tbsp. (8g)
- Luke warm water – ¾ cup (177ml)
- Olive oil – 3 tbsp. (45ml)
- Halved red grapes – 1 cup (150g)
- Rosemary – 2 tbsp. (14g)

### Method:

1. Add flour, active dry yeast, salt, and sugar to a mixing bowl and combine thoroughly.
2. The dry ingredients should be combined thoroughly with lukewarm water and olive oil.
3. The dough should be elastic and smooth after 10 minutes of kneading.
4. In a warm location, cover the dough and let it to rise for an hour.
5. Set the oven to 400°F.
6. Place the dough on a baking sheet that has been lined with parchment paper after rolling it out into a rectangle.

7. Grapes cut in half and rosemary are sprinkled on top of the dough.

8. Focaccia should be baked for 20 to 25 minutes, or until golden brown. Enjoy!

**Nutrition per serving:**
Calories - 211| Fat - 7g | Carbs - 33g | Protein - 4g | Sugar - 3g|Potassium - 72mg | Cholesterol – 0mg | Sodium – 292mg | Fiber – 1g

## 15.11 Homemade Italian Lemon Ice

Preparation Time: 10 minutes| Cooking Time: 0 minutes |Freezing Time: 3 hours |Serving: 6

**Ingredients:**

- Lemon juice – 1 cup (236ml)
- Water – 12 ounces (355ml)
- Granulated sugar – ½ cup (110g)
- Light corn syrup – ½ cup (118ml)
- Lemon zest – 1 tbsp. (3g)
- Salt – A pinch

**Method:**

1. Combine the water, sugar, corn syrup, lemon zest and salt in a medium saucepan. Stirring occasionally, cook over medium heat until the sugar has fully dissolved.

2. Remove from heat and mix in the lemon juice that has just been squeezed. Wait until the mixture reaches room temperature.

3. Place the mixture in a 9 × 13-inch baking dish and freeze it. Use a fork to smash any ice crystals that have developed after 30 minutes. Repeat this procedure every 30 minutes until the mixture has a fluffy, shaved-ice texture and is totally frozen (this should take around 2-3 hours).

4. Scoop the lemon ice into dishes for dishing, then devour right away.

**Nutrition per serving:** Calories - 148| Fat - 0g | Carbs - 39g | Protein - 0g | Sugar - 37g | Potassium - 58mg | Cholesterol – 0mg | Sodium – 29mg | Fiber – 1g

## 15.12 Vegan Apple Crisp

Preparation Time: 15 minutes | Cooking Time: 40 minutes | Serving: 4

### Ingredients

- Peeled apples – 4 medium
- Maple syrup – ¼ cup (59ml)
- Coconut sugar – ¼ cup (48g)
- All-purpose flour – ¼ cup (30g)
- Rolled oats – ¼ cup (20g)
- Almond flour – ¼ cup (28g)
- Chopped walnuts – ¼ cup (30g)
- Vegan butter – ¼ cup (60ml)
- Cinnamon – 1 tsp (8g)
- Nutmeg – ¼ tsp (0.5g)
- Salt – To Taste

### Method

1. Set the oven's temperature to 375°F (190°C).
2. Combine the apple slices, maple syrup, and coconut sugar in a large mixing basin. Mix well and reserve.
3. The all-purpose flour, rolled oats, almond flour, chopped walnuts, melted vegan butter, ground cinnamon, ground nutmeg, and a dash of salt should be combined in a separate mixing dish. Blend well until crumbly.
4. In a baking dish that is 9 inches square, pour the apple mixture. On top of the apple mixture, evenly distribute the crumbly mixture.
5. Bake for 35 to 40 minutes, or until the topping is golden brown and the apple mixture bubbles.
6. Before serving, take the apple crisp out of the oven and let it cool for a while.

### Nutrition per serving:

Calories - 338 | Fat - 16g | Carbs - 49g | Protein - 4g | Sugar - 33g | Potassium - 191mg | Cholesterol – 0mg | Sodium – 77mg | Fiber – 6g

# 16 SAUCES AND DRESSINGS

## 16.1 Nacho Sauce

Preparation Time - 2 minutes| Cooking Time - 12 minutes| Serves 1

**Ingredients:**

- Butter – 1 tbsp. (14.2g)
- Cheddar cheese (Shredded) – 8 oz (226.8g)
- All-purpose flour – 1 tbsp. (7.5g)
- Onion powder – ¼ tsp (0.5g)
- Garlic powder – ¼ tsp (0.6g)
- Almond milk – 1 cup (236.6ml)
- Salt & pepper – to taste

**Method:**

1. Melt the butter in a pan over medium heat.
2. Blend in the flour. Cook until light brown
3. Add the milk gradually while whisking, and heat until the sauce thickens
4. Stir in the shredded cheddar cheese, onion and garlic powders, salt, and pepper on low heat
5. Cook for 3-5 minutes, stirring regularly, until the cheese has melted and the sauce is smooth

**Nutrition per serving:** Calories - 157| Fat 11g| Carbs 5g| Protein 9g| Sugar 3g| Potassium 40mg

## 16.2 Tahini

Preparation Time - 2 minutes| Cooking Time - 12 minutes| Serves 1

**Ingredients:**

- Sesame seeds – 1 cup (144g)
- Salt – ¼ tsp (1.5g)
- Olive oil – ¼ cup (59ml)
- Water – as required
- Lemon juice – 2 tbsp. (30ml) (optional)

**Method:**

1. Turn on the oven to 350 °F (175 °C).
2. On a baking sheet, spread the sesame seeds uniformly, and bake for 5 to 10 minutes, or until lightly toasted
3. Let the seeds the cool
4. The sesame seeds should be added to a food processor and pulsed until they resemble crumbles
5. Salt and olive oil should be added to the processor and pulsed until the mixture is creamy and smooth.
6. Until you achieve the correct consistency, gradually add water to the mixture.
7. Add lemon juice to taste, if desired
8. Taste and adjust the seasoning.

**Nutrition per serving:** Calories - 109| Fat 10g| Carbs 3g| Protein 3g| Sugar 0g| Potassium 118mg

## 16.3 Hummus

Preparation Time - 2 minutes | Cooking Time - 12 minutes | Serves 1

### Ingredients:

- Chickpeas – 1 can (15oz/425g)
- Lemon juice – 3 tbsp. (44ml)
- Olive oil – ¼ cup (59ml)
- Tahini – 3 tbsp. (45g)
- Garlic cloves – 2
- Cumin (ground) – ½ tsp (1.55g)
- Salt – to taste
- Water – as required

### Method:

1. Combine the chickpeas, tahini, lemon juice, garlic, oil, cumin, and salt in a blender. till smooth
2. A tablespoon of water at a time can be added to the hummus if it is too thick to get the ideal consistency
3. Adjust the seasoning.
4. Add some olive oil to the hummus before placing it in a serving bowl. If desired, garnish with chopped parsley and paprika.

**Nutrition per serving:** Calories - 135 | Fat 1.4g | Carbs 8.5g | Protein 3.5g | Sugar 0g | Potassium 88mg

## 16.4 Guacamole

Preparation Time - 2 minutes | Cooking Time - 12 minutes | Serves 1

### Ingredients:

- Avocado – 2 medium sized
- Onion – ½ small sized
- Cilantro (chopped) – ¼ cup (4g)
- Tomato (chopped) – 1 small
- Garlic clove – 1
- Jalapeno pepper – 1 small
- Lemon juice – ½ lime
- Salt & pepper – to taste

### Method:

1. Remove the pit from the avocados and cut them in half. Put the flesh in a basin by scooping.
2. To the bowl with the avocado, add all ingredients
3. The mixture can be mashed to the appropriate consistency using a fork. You can smooth it out or keep it lumpy.
4. Adjust the seasoning.
5. To allow the flavors to mingle, place the dish in the refrigerator with the cover on for at least 30 minutes before serving.

### Nutrition per serving:

Calories - 155 | Fat 13g | Carbs 10g | Protein 2g | Sugar 1g | Potassium 485mg

## 16.5 Beetroot Hummus

Preparation Time - 7 minutes | Cooking Time - 0 minutes | Serves 3

### Ingredients:

- Beetroot (medium cooked) – 2
- Chickpea – 9 oz (255g)
- Garlic cloves – 2
- Olive oil – 2 tbsp. (28ml)
- Tahini – ¼ cup (60g)
- Salt – to taste
- Cumin – ½ tsp (1.15g)
- Lemon juice – ¼ cup (59ml)
- Water - as required

### Method:

1. To the bowl of a food processor, add the chickpeas, beetroots, tahini, lemon juice, garlic, salt, and cumin, run for a min or two
2. Add the olive oil in a thin stream while the food processor is running, and pulse the mixture until it is smooth.
3. If the mixture is too thick, add a tablespoon of water at a time until the required consistency is reached.
4. Adjust the seasoning.
5. The beetroot hummus can be consumed right away or kept in the refrigerator for up to five days if it is kept in an airtight container

**Nutrition per serving:** Calories - 214 | Fat 13g | Carbs 20g | Protein 6g | Sugar 0.2g | Potassium 205mg

## 16.6 Vegan Tzatziki

Preparation Time - 10 minutes | Cooking Time - 0 minutes | Serves 2

### Ingredients:

- Vegan yogurt – 1 cup (240g)
- Garlic cloves (minced) – 2
- Cucumber (grated) – 1 small
- Fresh mint (chopped) – 1 tbsp. (1g)
- Olive oil – 1 tbsp. (15ml)
- Fresh dill (chopped) – 1 tbsp. (3g)
- Lemon juice – 1 tbsp. (15ml)
- Salt & pepper – to taste

### Method:

1. The vegan yogurt, cucumber, garlic, dill, mint, lemon juice, and olive oil should all be combined in a mixing dish.
2. Mix thoroughly and add salt and pepper to taste.
3. To enable the flavors to mingle, cover and chill for at least 30 minutes.
4. Serve cold alongside crisp vegetables or pita bread.

### Nutrition per serving:

Calories - 66 | Fat 4g | Carbs 6g | Protein 2g | Sugar 4g | Potassium 125mg

## 16.7 Pumpkin Chili dressing

Preparation Time - 10 minutes | Cooking Time - 30 minutes | Serves 5

### Ingredients:

- Pumpkin puree – 1 can (15oz/443ml)
- Black beans – 1 can (15oz/425g)
- Tomatoes (diced) – 4
- Green chilies – 2 medium sized
- Onion (diced) – ¼ cup (45g)
- Cheddar cheese (shredded) – 4 oz. (113g)
- Garlic cloves (minced) – 2
- Cumin – ½ tsp (1.1g)
- Chili powder – 2 tsp (5.2g)
- Salt & pepper – to taste

### Method:

1. Set your oven's temperature to 375°F (190°C)
2. Add pumpkin puree, black beans, diced tomatoes with green chilies, cheddar cheese, diced onion, minced garlic, chili powder, cumin, salt, and pepper in a bowl and blend thoroughly
3. Fill a 9-inch (23 cm) baking dish with the ingredients
4. The dip should be baked for 25–30 minutes, or until hot and bubbling
5. Provide warm tortilla chips or vegetable sticks with the pumpkin chili dip

**Nutrition per serving:** Calories - 208 | Fat 11g | Carbs 19g | Protein 9g | Sugar 3g | Potassium 95mg

## 16.8 Vegan Pate

Preparation Time - 10 minutes | Cooking Time - 12 minutes | Serves 2

### Ingredients:

- Walnuts – 1 cup (100g)
- Mushrooms (chopped) – ½ cup (50g)
- Garlic clove (minced) – 1
- Onions (chopped) – ½ cup (85g)
- Nutritional yeast – 2 tbsp. (12g)
- Soy sauce – 1 tbsp. (15ml)
- Olive oil – 2 tbsp. (30ml)
- Dried thyme – ¼ tsp (0.26g)

### Method:

1. Turn on the oven to 350°F (180°C)
2. The raw walnuts should be spread out on a baking sheet and toasted in the oven for 10 to 12 minutes, or until aromatic and lightly browned
3. The chopped mushrooms, chopped onion, and minced garlic should be sautéed in olive oil over medium heat until the mushrooms are soft
4. Add the nutritional yeast, soy sauce, lemon juice, dried thyme, salt, and black pepper to the food processor along with the toasted walnuts and mushroom combination that has been sautéed. Pulse the mixture until it is thoroughly blended and has a smooth, creamy texture
5. After tasting, adjust the seasoning as necessary

6. Place the pate dip in the refrigerator to chill for at least 30 minutes before serving

**Nutrition per serving:** Calories - 174| Fat 16g| Carbs 6g| Protein 5g| Sugar 2g| Potassium 105mg

## 16.9 Vegan Avocado & Coconut sauce

Preparation Time - 7 minutes| Cooking Time - 0 minutes| Serves 1

**Ingredients:**

- Coconut cream – ½ cup (120g)
- Avocado – 1 ripe
- Cilantro – 1 tbsp. (3g)
- Garlic cloves – 1
- Lime juice – 1 tbsp. (15ml)
- Salt & pepper – to taste

**Method:**

1. Remove the avocado's pit, cut it in half, and scoop the flesh into a bowl
2. Coriander, lime juice, minced garlic, and coconut cream should all be added to the bowl
3. The ingredients should be thoroughly blended and mashed together using a fork
4. Add salt and pepper to the food as desired
5. Place the dip in a serving basin and, if like, top with more cilantro
6. Serve alongside crackers or your preferred vegetables

**Nutrition per serving:** Calories - 120| Fat 11g| Carbs 6g| Protein 1g| Sugar 1g| Potassium 125mg

## 16.10 Sweet Potato sauce

Preparation Time - 10 minutes| Cooking Time - 30 minutes| Serves 1

**Ingredients:**

- Greek yogurt – ¼ cup (60g)
- Sweet potatoes (peeled & cubed) – 2 medium sized
- Garlic cloves (minced) – 2
- Olive oil – 2 tbsp. (30ml)
- Smoked paprika – 1 tsp (2g)
- Salt & pepper – to taste

**Method:**

1. Set the oven's temperature to 400°F (200°C)
2. Sprinkle olive oil over the sweet potato cubes before placing them on a baking dish. To taste, add salt and pepper to the food
3. Roast the sweet potatoes for 25 to 30 minutes, or until they are cooked through and have a light browning
4. After letting the sweet potatoes cool for a short while, add them to a food processor
5. To the food processor, add the minced garlic, Greek yogurt, smoked paprika, and a dash of salt and pepper
6. The mixture should be smooth and creamy after blending
7. Taste the dip and make any required seasoning adjustments

**Nutrition per serving:** Calories - 77| Fat 3.8g| Carbs 9.3g| Protein 1.5g| Sugar 2.8g| Potassium 205mg

## 16.11 Bean Dip

Preparation Time - 10 minutes | Cooking Time - 20 minutes | Serves 5

### Ingredients:

- Black beans – 1 can (15 oz)
- Pinto beans – 1 can (15 oz)
- Red onion – ½ medium sized
- Corn – 1 can (15 oz)
- Green bell pepper – ½ medium sized
- Red bell pepper – ½ medium sized
- Garlic cloves (minced) – 2
- Cumin – 1 tsp (2.5g)
- Black pepper – ¼ tsp (0.6g)
- Salt – ½ tsp (2.5g)
- Chili powder – 1 tbsp. (8g)
- Olive oil – 2 tbsp. (30ml)
- Lime juice – 2 tbsp. (30ml)
- Fresh cilantro – 2 tbsp. (6g)
- Cheese – for topping

### Method:

1. Set the oven's temperature to 350°F (175°C)
2. Olive oil should be heated in a sizable skillet over medium heat
3. When the vegetables are tender, add the diced red onion, red pepper, and green pepper to the skillet and cook for about 5 minutes
4. When the spices are fragrant, add the minced garlic, chili powder, cumin, salt, and black pepper to the skillet and stir for about a minute
5. Stir together the black beans, pinto beans and corn after they have been washed and drained
6. Stir together the lime juice and chopped cilantro in the skillet
7. The mixture should be transferred to a 9 x 13 baking dish
8. Bake for 15-20 minutes, or until the dip is thoroughly cooked and the top is golden
9. Serve with chips and cheese topping

**Nutrition per serving:** Calories - 153 | Fat 5.4g | Carbs 23.6g | Protein 6.9g | Sugar 2.8g | Potassium 260mg

## 16.12 Tamarind sauce

Preparation Time - 7 minutes | Cooking Time - 15 minutes | Serves 1

### Ingredients:

- Tamarind paste – ½ cup (175g)
- Brown sugar – ¼ cup (50g)
- Water – ¼ cup (60ml)
- Salt – 1 tsp (5.7g)
- Cumin powder – ½ tsp (1.25g)
- Chili powder – ½ tsp (1.5g)
- Four seed kernels – 1 tsp (3g)

### Method:

1. The tamarind paste, brown sugar, water, salt, cumin powder, and red chili powder should all be combined in a medium pot. To blend, thoroughly stir
2. Over medium-high heat, bring the mixture to a boil. Then, turn the heat down to low and simmer the mixture, stirring regularly, for 10 to 15 minutes, or until it thickens

3. Remove the dip from the heat and allow it to cool to room temperature
4. Add some 4 seed kernels if you like

**Nutrition per serving:** Calories - 27| Fat 0g| Carbs 7g| Protein 0g| Sugar 6g| Potassium 75mg

## 16.13 Mango sauce

Preparation Time - 15 minutes| Cooking Time - 0 minutes| Serves 3

### Ingredients:

- Mangoes (peeled & diced) – 2 ripe
- Red onion – ¼ cup (40g)
- Fresh cilantro – ¼ cup (15g)
- Jalapeno pepper (minced) – 1
- Salt & pepper – to taste

### Method:

1. Diced mango, red onion, cilantro, and jalapeño pepper should all be combined in a medium bowl
2. Add salt and pepper, then squeeze the juice of 1 lime over the mixture
3. Blend all ingredients for at least 15 minutes, and serve fresh for better taste

**Nutrition per serving:** Calories - 57| Fat 0.3g| Carbs 14.7g| Protein 0.8g| Sugar 12.2g| Potassium 187mg

## 16.14 Gochujang dip

Preparation Time - 5 minutes| Cooking Time - 0 minutes| Serves 2

### Ingredients:

- Gochujang – 3 tbsp. (45ml)
- Soy sauce – 1 tbsp. (15ml)
- Honey – 2 tbsp. (30ml)
- Garlic clove – 1
- Rice vinegar – 1 tbsp. (15ml)

### Method:

1. Whisk all the ingredients in a bowl until thoroughly blended
2. Taste the sauce and make any required spice adjustments. To increase sweetness or spice, you can add extra honey or gochujang
3. The sauce can be used right once or kept in the refrigerator for up to a week in an airtight container

**Nutrition per serving:** Calories - 27| Fat - 0g| Carbs - 7g| Protein - 1g| Sugar - 0g| Potassium - 60mg

# 17 10-WEEK HEALTHY VEGAN

Here is a **10-Week Healthy Vegan** meal plan with different menus suggested by a licensed dietitian. Each week includes 3 large meals and 2 snacks, along with the caloric distribution for each meal. Please note that the calorie needs may vary from person to person based on their age, gender, weight, and physical activity level. This meal plan is designed to provide approximately **1200-1600** calories per day.

**Week 1:**
- **Breakfast: 7.1** Whole Wheat Pancakes (327 calories)
- **Snack: 8.12** Avocado and Mango Salad (301 calories)
- **Lunch: 10.4** Classic Tomato Soup (362 calories)
- **Snack: 14.1** Blueberry Banana Smoothie (220 calories)
- **Dinner: 9.4** Veg Tofu Bowl (380 calories)
- **TOTAL – 1590 Calories**

**Week 2:**
- **Breakfast: 7.2** Classic French Toast (498 calories)
- **Snack: 8.7** Quinoa and Chickpea Salad (348 calories)
- **Lunch: 10.1** Potato and Carrot Stew (146 calories)
- **Snack: 14.3** Detoxifying Green Machine (180 calories)
- **Dinner: 9.8** Parmesan Eggplant Bowl (363 calories)
- **TOTAL – 1535 Calories**

**Week 3:**
- **Breakfast: 7.3** Oatmeal with fruits and Nuts (334 calories)
- **Snack: 8.11** Beet and Quinoa Salad (354 calories)
- **Lunch: 8.16** Potato Salad (200 calories)
- **Snack: 14.2** Peach Raspberry smoothie (200 calories)
- **Dinner: 11.4** Vegan Mushroom Risotto (447 calories)
- **TOTAL – 1535 Calories**

**Week 4:**
- **Breakfast: 7.4** Avocado Toast (415 calories)
- **Snack: 8.15** Tuscan and White Bean Salad (214 calories)
- **Lunch: 10.7** Classic Lentil Soup (217 calories)
- **Snack: 12.1** Hunarian Paprika Potatoes (252 calories)
- **Dinner: 11.8** Vegetable Quinoa Fried Rice (342 calories)
- **TOTAL – 1440 Calories**

**Week 5:**
- **Breakfast:** **7.5** Oats and Chia Pudding (344 calories)
- **Snack:** **8.10** Edamame and Tofu Salad (274 calories)
- **Lunch:** **10.8** Minestrone Soup (191 calories)
- **Snack:** **14.11** Turmeric Pineapple Smoothie (195 calories)
- **Dinner:** **11.9** Vegetable Sphagetti Bolognese (385 calories)
- **TOTAL – 1389 Calories**

**Week 6:**
- **Breakfast:** **7.6** Scrambled Tofu and Mushroom Omelet (198 calories)
- **Snack:** **8.7** Quinoa and Chickpea Salad (348 calories)
- **Lunch:** **12.9** Temph Tacos (318 calories)
- **Snack:** **8.12** Avocado and Mango Salad (230 calories)
- **Dinner:** **11.13** Vegetable One-Pot Pasta (455 calories)
- **TOTAL – 1549 Calories**

**Week 7:**
- **Breakfast:** **7.7** Banana and Peanut Butter Muffin (637 calories)
- **Snack:** **8.14** Arugula and Fennel Salad (140 calories)
- **Lunch:** **10.9** Butternut Squash Soup (121 calories)
- **Snack:** **14.10** Ginger Fruity Smoothie (87 calories)
- **Dinner:** **11.6** Mushroom and Vegetable Wild Rice Pilaf (299 calories)
- **TOTAL – 1284 Calories**

**Week 8:**
- **Breakfast:** **7.8** Avocado and Chickpea Pancakes 295 calories)
- **Snack:** **8.6** Tomato Spinach Salad (202 calories)
- **Lunch:** **10.14** Mushroom Stew (202 calories)
- **Snack:** **14.12** Cherry Chocolate Smoothie (267 calories)
- **Dinner:** **11.10** Vegetable Fettuccine Alfredo (623 calories)
- **TOTAL – 1589 Calories**

**Week 9:**
- **Breakfast:** **7.10** Scrambled Tofu Wrap (385 calories)
- **Snack:** **8.4** Corn and Black Bean Salad (197 calories)
- **Lunch:** **10.12** Vegetable and Farro Soup (212 calories)
- **Snack:** **14.9** Berry Blast Smoothie (307 calories)
- **Dinner:** **11.20** Spicy Veggie Ramen with Tofu (297 calories)
- **TOTAL – 1398 Calories**

**Week 10:**
- **Breakfast:** **7.19** Granola Yogurt Parfait (380 calories)
- **Snack:** **8.3** Tofu Salad (256 calories)
- **Lunch:** **10.11** Gazpacho and Tomato Soup (153 calories)
- **Snack:** **14.6** Mango Pineapple Smoothie (260 calories)
- **Dinner:** **11.17** Black Bean Chili Quinoa (388 calories)
- **TOTAL – 1437 Calories**

# 18 CONCLUSION

In conclusion, this Plant-Based Diet Cookbook has provided you with the tools, knowledge, and inspiration needed to embrace and thrive on a plant-based lifestyle. With the help of this cookbook, you can explore the wonderful world of plant-based eating with ease and confidence. From nutrient-dense breakfasts to hearty dinners, this cookbook offers a wide range of recipes that are both satisfying and nourishing. In addition, the guide to plant-based and vegan approaches, kitchen equipment, and storage tips make it easy to navigate this lifestyle with ease. As a nutritionist and dietitian with years of experience, my goal has always been to guide and support individuals on their journey towards optimal health, while simultaneously nurturing their passion for food and culinary exploration. As you continue to incorporate more plant-based meals into your routine, remember to focus on whole, minimally processed ingredients that provide an abundance of nutrients and flavors. By doing so, you will not only reap the personal health benefits but also contribute to a more sustainable and compassionate world. I encourage you to experiment with the recipes in this cookbook and make them your own. Embrace the diversity of plant-based ingredients, and don't be afraid to adapt the dishes to suit your personal preferences and dietary needs. Adopting a plant-based diet is not only a healthy choice, but also an affordable and delicious one. So, whether you are a seasoned vegan or just starting out, this cookbook is a must-have for anyone looking to improve their health and well-being through plant-based eating. Say goodbye to fancy diets and hello to a sustainable and delicious way of eating. I hope this cookbook has left you feeling empowered and excited about the endless possibilities of plant-based cooking. Remember, a vibrant, nourishing, and delicious future is within your reach. So let's raise a fork and toast to your continued success on this plant-based journey. Here's to a vibrant, nourishing, and delicious future.

LINK TO DOWNLOAD THE BONUS: https://dl.bookfunnel.com/8qwhc3g876

# MEASUREMENTS

| Volume Equivalents (Dry) | |
|---|---|
| **US STANDARD** | **METRIC (APPROX.)** |
| 1/8 teaspoon | 0.5 mL |
| 1/4 teaspoon | 1 mL |
| 1/2 teaspoon | 2 mL |
| 3/4 teaspoon | 4 mL |
| 1 teaspoon | 5 mL |
| 1 tablespoon | 15 mL |
| 1/4 cup | 59 mL |
| 1/2 cup | 118 mL |
| 3/4 cup | 177 mL |
| 1 cup | 235 mL |
| 2 cups | 475 mL |
| 3 cups | 700 mL |
| 4 cups | 1 L |

| Volume Equivalents (Liquid) | | |
|---|---|---|
| **US STANDARD** | **US STANDARD (OUNCES)** | **METRIC (APPROX.)** |
| 2 tablespoons | 1 fl. oz. | 30 mL |
| 1/4 cup | 2 fl. oz. | 60 mL |
| 1/2 cup | 4 fl. oz. | 120 mL |
| 1 cup | 8 fl. oz. | 240 mL |
| 1 1/2 cup | 12 fl. oz. | 355 mL |
| 2 cups or 1 pint | 16 fl. oz. | 475 mL |
| 4 cups or 1 quart | 32 fl. oz. | 1 L |
| 1 gallon | 128 fl. oz. | 4 L |

| Weight Equivalents | |
|---|---|
| **US STANDARD** | **METRIC (APPROXIMATE)** |
| 1 ounce | 28 g |
| 2 ounces | 57 g |
| 5 ounces | 142 g |
| 10 ounces | 284 g |
| 15 ounces | 425 g |
| 16 ounces (1 pound) | 455 g |
| 1.5 pounds | 680 g |
| 2 pounds | 907 g |

| Temperature Equivalents | |
|---|---|
| **FAHR.(F)** | **METRIC (APPROX.)** |
| 225 °F | 107 °C |
| 250 °F | 120 °C |
| 275 °F | 135 °C |
| 300 °F | 150 °C |
| 325 °F | 160 °C |
| 350 °F | 180 °C |
| 375 °F | 190 °C |
| 400 °F | 205 °C |
| 425 °F | 220 °C |
| 450 °F | 235 °C |
| 475 °F | 245 °C |
| 500 °F | 260 °C |

Printed in Great Britain
by Amazon